LANDSLIDE!

How Big Ideas Win Big Majorities

(And Have Done for the Last 120 Years)

by

CHRIS WEST

'Initium ut esset, homo creatus est.'

('Humanity was created to make new things')

St Augustine

To

Gervas Huxley, who believed in this book from the start

Published by CWTK Publications

Cover design by 100covers

Contents

Introduction

So, what is a Political Programme?   1

Science: an Inspiration   16

Rise and Fall   26

The Model in Action   57

    New Liberalism   60

    The Knock-out Blow   72

    A Land Fit for Heroes   78

    Tranquillity   84

    1945 Socialism   96

    One Nation   106

    White Heat   117

    The 1970s   129

    Thatcherism   139

    New Labour   152

    Coalition   163

    Populist 'Brexit' Nationalism 168

    A New Deal?   183

Conclusion   193

Ten Quick Tips for the Ambitious   196

Appendices

    Some Critiques of the Model 199

    The Big Ideas   206

    Glossary   209

    UK elections, 1906 to 2019 216

    The Body-blows   218

    The Eras: A Playlist   220

Principal References   222

Acknowledgements   226

Introduction

British politics is at a moment of crisis. One administration has run out of steam. The next is still in waiting, still unsure exactly what it believes. Meanwhile, all around us, change is accelerating.

Scary. But we have been here before. Administrations rise and fall; they always have. I wrote this book to try and make sense of this process, to lessen that feeling of hurtling into a dark tunnel and, instead, understand that this is all part of something (reasonably) regular and predictable.

To do this, I had to build a model. After some dead ends and a lot of tinkering, I present it in this book.

At its heart is what I call a Political Programme. I'll go into lots more detail in the next chapter, but for now, this is a set of plans and policies built around a powerful new vision. It is timely: it captures a rising new *Zeitgeist*. This timeliness gives it *cultural power* – it excites people; it gives them energy and conviction. This is then turned into *political power*, the culmination of which is a Landslide victory in a general election – hence the title of this book.

A triumph! But the Wheel of Fortune keeps turning. Ultimately the cultural power begins to wane, as times change but the nature of the Programme, forged in a particular historical moment, does not (and cannot). Various things go wrong – usually climaxing in one big disaster. Loss of political power follows – though Programmes that have lost their cultural power but still have a majority in the House can limp along for a long time. They are doomed, however: the last dinosaurs shivering in a post-asteroid world.

A new Programme will soon arise to replace it, however. Human beings are too creative and ambitious to let political vacuums last long.

I shall seek to show that this cycle has repeated itself – with slight differences, as human affairs never fit totally rigid models – ten times since the start of the last century.

I begin by describing a Political Programme. What is it, exactly? There is a powerful analogy with science, thanks to its ongoing story of competing Big Ideas.

I then attempt to model the life-cycle that a Political Programme goes through. Then I shall show this model in action via the stories of the ten cycles that we have seen since 1900. I shall say where I think the cycle has currently got to.

Finally, I shall outline a possible Political Programme for the rest of the 2020s. This is beyond the essentially descriptive brief of the book, but I can't resist it. The moment insists.

I know this approach is unfashionable. It's a Grand Narrative, and we're not supposed to do Grand Narratives any longer. Ah, well, I've never been a *fashionista*. I hope this book will inform, entertain, reassure and, most of all, inspire positive change.

So, what is a Political Programme?

So, what is this thing I call a Political Programme? It has a number of characteristics.

- It is Original and Timely. The latter gives it Cultural Power
- It converts its Cultural Power into Political Success
- It consists of Models, Values, Stories and Core Policies…
- …constellated around a clear, simple Big Idea.

That might look appallingly dry, so let's look at each of these aspects in more detail and bring them to life.

Original

A Political Programme is a new way of looking at the world and a new set of responses to what is seen. It isn't just sticking a shiny new label on old policies, or giving old stuff 'one more heave'. It isn't doing the direct opposite to what 'the other lot' did, either – do that, and you've made no progress conceptually. Political Programmes create fresh arguments, not just shout louder in old ones.

An analogy from business: Political Programmes create Blue Oceans. This term was coined by W Chan Kim and Renée Mauborgne, two professors at INSEAD, the global business school near Paris. They were not talking about party colours, but about an approach to business strategy where it is not a matter of outperforming rivals but of seeing and doing things so differently that those rivals become 'irrelevant'. A good example is IKEA, who totally reinvented how we buy furniture (out of town; a guided 'buyer journey'; standardized flat-pack products you take home – and you get meatballs). Kim and Mauborgne contrast this with Red Oceans, so called because they are red with the blood of combatants fighting over existing, clearly defined territory – for example, two old-fashioned furniture shops with their overeager salespeople, endless customization, long waits for delivery and not a meatball in sight, battling it out in the same high street.

(Kim and Mauborgne go on to outline a method for creating Blue Oceans. While it's interesting, I feel there are better models for political innovation – all analogies break down at some point.)

Blue Oceans take time to establish, in commerce and in politics. New and evolving Political Programmes may be ignored or frowned on to start with, just as people first sneered at IKEA. By contrast, in their prime, or 'Pomp' as I call it, they are assumed to be right on a huge range of issues. "There is no alternative," its leaders proclaim, and listeners nod wistfully and think, 'If only there were!' There *are* always alternatives, of course, but the Cultural Power of the Programme has temporarily obscured that fact.

At the same time, a Political Programme is never a *total* reinvention – any more than a Blue Ocean business is. We still end up after our trip to IKEA with tables, beds, bookcases and chairs (though we may have used a few expletives assembling them). The new Programme will also contain some content *carried forward* from old ones. I shall look at that non-radical aspect of change at the end of this chapter.

Timely
Eras change. So do the spirits that go with them – their *Zeitgeist*. Look at almost any TV sitcom over thirty years old – there are loads on YouTube – and it won't be long before you start grimacing. No doubt people in

2053 will look at the material that we enjoy today and experience the same feeling of unease. (At which aspects? Such is the adventure of cultural change: right now, we haven't a clue.)

Era-change does not take place at an even pace. Author Douglas B Holt compares the process to punctuated equilibrium in evolution. Given some new opportunity, species evolve relatively quickly, to seize it then maximize their fitness for it. The ancestors of modern mammals evolved speedily after the dinosaurs disappeared. Well-adapted, they then stay constant, often for a very long time. Sharks have been bossing our oceans for over 400 million years. Finally, they disappear, fast by evolutionary standards, as environmental changes suddenly make their well-honed natures and habits unsupportable. Giant insects thrived 255 million years ago but all vanished in a giant mass extinction. Holt argues that the same happens to our cultural eras and their spirits. Meteoric and attention-grabbing to start with, they then enjoy a longish period of dominance, before suffering a sudden collapse into irrelevance as the world changes and people's needs and perceptions change with it.

Political Programmes are inextricably bound up with this process of era-change. They catch the spirit of a new era in its rising phase. They then become part of the rise of that spirit – Margaret Thatcher wasn't just a policymaker but a moving spirit of 80s culture. A self-reinforcing spiral (a 'positive feedback loop' in the language of systems theory) comes into being, of national mood-change and a Programme's input. A cultural wave results, which the Programme rides to glory.

However, in time the wave collapses. The Programme may be part of the reason for that collapse – the 1963 Profumo affair didn't just destroy a Political Programme, but changed a national mood.

Some thinkers have argued that politicians create eras on their own. Victorian historian Thomas Carlyle believed that history was static until kicked into action by Great Men (no Great Women; such was his era). This seems to overrate politicians' – or any individual's – power.

No, history is ever-changing and 'greatness' is inextricably bound up with timing. There is a window of opportunity to create era-defining positive feedback loops, when an old mood is dead or stale and a new mood is beginning to form. Ideas too far ahead of their era will be unable to develop momentum (though if the proponents wait long enough and keep promoting their message, the opportunity may suddenly appear). Too late, and events have already moved on.

There is something of ancient Chinese philosophy in this. The Book of Changes (*Yijing* or *I Ching*) contains 64 model moments – illustrated by 'hexagrams' – all of which require different balances of courage and caution. An action that is a masterstroke when one of these model moments is in the ascendant can be meaningless or even folly when another of the 64 moments is.

Cultural Power

A Programme's Timeliness gives it Cultural Power.

The concept of Cultural Power originated with the mid-20th century Italian philosopher Antonio Gramsci. However, his model, with its Marxian roots, places culture in a bigger structure of Capitalist power and class struggle. My own sense of culture is less formal and more unpredictable. Cultural Power isn't granted by 'the system'; it has to be striven for.

Cultural Power isn't just about artefacts: music, novels, movies, fashion (and so on). It's about how people see themselves and the world. This is partly intellectual but also emotional. It's about belonging. It's about energy. A Programme with Cultural Power makes voters say "Yes!" and "At last, someone is speaking up for people like me!" and "Finally, people who see things my way!" This wins it diehard fans, fans for life, like pensioners who get misty-eyed listening to The Beatles. It once gave them a voice, an identity, and they will never forget that. 'Rock'n'roll will never die,' say veterans of that era. 'Thatcherism will never die,' say Conservatives who came of age in the 1980s.

Cultural Power ripples out beyond these true enthusiasts to people who are less starry-eyed but still sign up to the Programme and its culture with a smile. But it's the fans who drive it.

Political Success

A Political Programme achieves legislative and executive power, and keeps that power for a decent length of time. In UK politics, this comes via a substantial victory in a general election, a Landslide. Only such victories allow a Programme fully to put its ideas into practice.

All Political Programmes start off as *Aspirant* ones. Most of these fall into various 'chasms' that I shall discuss later, and never achieve Landslides. Some fail quickly – examples include the Common Wealth Party that held five seats in the 1940s, and the Natural Law Party that fielded 310 candidates in the 1992 election (all of whom lost their deposits). Others, more intriguingly, manage to get one hand on the levers of power but never manage to turn that into full-on control. Examples there include Ramsay MacDonald's 1920s Socialism and 'Orange Book' Liberalism (more on them in the history section of this book).

Only a fortunate few make it to real power.

In British politics, a full-on, successful Political Programme almost always takes the form of self-reinvention by one of the two major parties. The one exception was the rise of Labour in the first half of the twentieth century, which started the century with no seats at all but slowly rose to replace the once-mighty Liberals. Right now, however, it seems more likely that if a new party does appear, it will end up getting osmosed into one of the current big two – which will be a huge victory for the newcomer in terms of policy, though the rosettes of the candidates will still be red or blue. The Brexit Party did this to the Conservatives in 2019.

Liberal Democrat readers will no doubt disagree.

So, that's what a Political Programme looks like and does. Let's look under the bonnet and see what it is made of.

Models
A Political Programme has its own Models. These are its big pictures of how the world works: economics, sociology, psychology, geopolitics, technology, (in the future, hopefully) ecology. Religion and a specific theory of history may also form a part.

Different types of Model will weigh more powerfully than others for different Programmes. Thatcherism was not interested in sociology but driven by economics. The Programme I call '1945 Socialism' was the other way round, with social class at the heart of its thinking.

Psychology is an interesting one. Theorizing about 'human nature' is even more unfashionable than Grand Narratives, but scratch most political theories and you will find assumptions about what people desire or need. How improvable are we? How altruistic?

Models include metrics. What does success look – or, more important, feel – like? What target, if hit, will silence doubters and fill Programme supporters with unquenchable pride? Victory in battle? Empire? Greater equality? Economic growth? Sovereignty? A rise in Gross National Happiness?

Politicians who claim to be simply pragmatic and free of any such big pictures are deceiving us (and themselves, too). No political thought takes place in a conceptual vacuum.

Values
Models are about how the world works; Values are about how it should work.

Values almost always play a role in choosing Models. Back in 1739, philosopher David Hume said that we shouldn't do this. We cannot derive 'ought' statements from statements of fact, he said. Philosophy departments still insist on this distinction. Everywhere else, people ignore it. Anna Killick's recent book *Politicians and Economic Experts* shows how politicians of all shades choose economic models that fit their emotional convictions about the relative values of equality, class, community, freedom, hard work, enterprise (and so on).

In theory, this opens the door to relativism. In practice, way-out Models soon collapse under the pressure of reality. Governments of all shades (unless they're led by Liz Truss and Kwasi Kwarteng) listen to experts. The most productive arguments are practical and fact-based – though people enter those arguments with sets of Values and usually leave them with those Values unchanged.

Models and Values are best illustrated via…

Stories

Our ancestors lived – and our social emotions evolved – in tribes or clans, where Models and Values were inculcated through shared narratives. As they sat at the feet of their elders, maybe round a fire with the infinite star-filled sky above them, youngsters listened to stories, and through these stories learnt answers to huge questions. How does the world work? What sort of people do what sort of things? What are the consequences of those actions? Where do I fit in to all that? How do I become one of the good guys?

Political Programmes do the same. They use two essential types of story.

The first is about Dragon-slaying:

- Something of great value…

- …is under dire threat from a malign force (or forces)

- Fear not! The Programme will come to the rescue.

The second type is about the Bright Future that the Programme will build once the Dragon is slain and things are done the way the Programme says they should be.

Dragon-slaying Stories teem with characters. There are *Villains*: bullying, exploiting, gaming the system, standing in the way of Progress or Justice or National Pride (or some other Big Value). There are *Victims*, decent folk suffering as a result of this villainy. Enter the *Heroes* (of either gender, though they tended to be male in older Programmes) to the rescue!

Among the Victims, there will be special ones – the Programme's Archetypes. These people will have similar Models and Values to the Programme. It is in their name that the Programme is fighting, and it will call out to them especially to rise up and join it in defeating the Villains. They will, the Programme hopes, respond at the ballot box – but more: they will do so in their lives, turning into fans who get out there and argue for the Programme, on Facebook, in front rooms, in pubs, social clubs, Women's Institutes, churches (and so on) up and down the country. The most determined will end up in the front row on *Question Time*, glaring at the panel representative of the old, dying Programme and rousing the audience to applause when they fire rhetoric-laden questions at them.

Second, <u>Bright-Future Stories</u> are less dramatic but should be the real long-term point of a Political Programme. With the Villains vanquished, the heroic Programme sets to work creating the Bright Future (bright for everyone, of course, except for the Villains)(and especially bright for the Archetypes).

Some Political Programmes are essentially about Dragon-slaying. Lloyd George's 1916 Programme was, unsurprisingly, mostly concerned with defeating the German Imperial state on the field of battle. These are the easiest narratives to create and sell.

Other Programmes put more stress on Bright Futures. Lloyd George's second Programme, after victory in November 1918, sought to create 'A Fit Country for Heroes to Live in'.

Thatcherism provides an example of a strong mixture of Stories, both pursued with intensity. The trade unions, government bureaucracy and the far left were the Dragons in need of slaying. Entrepreneurs and other wealth-creators were the heroic makers of (and beneficiaries from) the Bright Future.

Both sets of Stories will have their own coded language, so the audience can cheer or boo at the right moments ('Bolsheviks', 'Guilty Men', 'the loony left', 'hard-working families', 'patriots', 'remoaners').

The Programme's Models, Values and Stories go to make up its *Worldview*, and are what give it Cultural Power.

Core Policies

We now leave the world of Cultural Power for the specifics of policy. How, exactly, will the Dragon be slain? How, precisely, will the Bright Future be built? The Programme's founders will create an *Action Plan*, a list of *Core Policies,* prioritized in order of urgency. These will be substantial, and some will be radical.

Core Policies *must* be implemented for a Programme to be fulfilled. A Programme that does a U-turn on a Core Policy has failed. To quote Enoch Powell, a man now rightly criticized for his views on race but who had a profound understanding of the political process: "It is fatal for any government... to seek to govern in direct opposition to the principles with which they were entrusted with the right to govern."

This does not mean that a Political Programme has *no* room for flexibility. Far from it. As long as it sticks to its Worldview and Core Policies, it can improvise as much as it likes. It can test, tinker with and drop *non-core* policies to meet changing circumstances. Indeed, it must do so. Change is perpetual, and every administration has to come up with responses to these changes. But it cannot do so by ditching its Worldview or Core Policies, otherwise it stands for nothing. Flexibility within an inflexible framework: such is the art of politics in this model.

A Big Idea

This is the distilled essence of the Programme. Lovers of literature may like to think of the Big Idea as the underlying theme of a work. For film buffs, it's what screenwriting guru Robert McKee calls the 'controlling idea' of a movie. I like the metaphor of its being the sun around which the Models, Values, Stories and Core Policies orbit.

It is simple. It can be just a word or a phrase. 'Tranquillity' was a Big Idea for the previously warlike Conservatives in the early 1920s. Clement Attlee's Socialist Britain was a Big Idea (Socialism itself was no new idea, of course, but Attlee's Programme had a particular way of putting it into practice). Margaret Thatcher's Enterprise Economy was a Big Idea. New Labour was a Big Idea. Brexit was a Big Idea. People hear the Idea and know that this is fresh and that lots of new things will flow from it.

This simplicity is terribly unfair. A Big Idea is like a great melody. You can think, 'My God, that's beautiful' and at the same time, 'It's just a few notes. Why the hell didn't I think of that? I could be playing 80,000-seater stadia, not doing my usual Saturday night gig at the Dog and Duck!' (But you didn't. Time to go and set up, and don't forget that the punters do *not* want original material.)

In considering Big Ideas, I find it helpful to add a few sentences to the word or phrase, expanding it a little to outline core concerns and policies or the general 'feel' of the Programme. So, for example, I adumbrate New Liberalism (the first new Big Idea of the 20th century) by adding: 'The poorest people in the UK are trapped in poverty, and only the state can remedy this. We will set up a German-style welfare system to enable them to escape this trap and lead more fulfilling lives. We will pay for it

11

with income and land taxes, not import tariffs, as free trade creates wealth.'

These sentences are equivalent to the 'elevator pitch' of a start-up business. In this metaphor, the entrepreneur gets into a lift and there's one other person in there – the exact individual they have been looking to pitch their idea to. This person presses 'six' and the lift begins to move. The entrepreneur has those six floors to convince them. And only six floors. The lift doesn't get stuck. She or he can't hand the target an eighty-page business plan, either: it won't get read. In a few sentences, what will grab the attention and interest of the target?

In politics, we're more likely to be on a doorstep than in a lift. What do we say when the person who answers our knock asks, "What are you lot going to do this time?" Or "So, what's the Big Idea?"

"No!" shout critics of the above. "Simplistic solutions can do untold damage!"

Yes, some Big Ideas have caused appalling damage. Communism and Naziism, again. But that just shows that there are bad Big Ideas, unimaginably bad ones, not that all Big Ideas are bad.

19th century military philosopher Carl von Clausewitz wrote: 'Determination in carrying through a simple idea is the surest way to achieve success.'

In the next chapter, I shall show that Science has a similar logical structure: it is driven by Big Ideas that are conceptually profound, deeply radical and annoyingly (to other people in the field, wrestling with the difficulty of it all) simple.

Big Ideas vs. Slogans

Part of the reason why thoughtful people distrust the 'Big Idea' concept is that they confuse Big Ideas with Slogans.

Slogans are superficial attention-grabbers. Harold Wilson's 1960s 'White Heat' Programme was based on a resonant, original Big Idea that Britain was stuck in an economic and cultural rut created by the old class system, and would be jolted out of it, economically by unleashing the power of science, planning and technology, and culturally by making national life less stuffy and more open and varied. Plenty to get stuck into there. The election Slogan that went with it in 1964 was 'Let's go with Labour!' Go where? How? The slogan didn't say. It didn't need to. It grabbed attention; it created a mood, one of energy. Job done. Time to move on to the serious stuff.

Politicians and their supporters can get into trouble confusing the two. They can mouth Slogans and convince themselves that they have a Big Idea. When they start trying to put the Slogan into action, they find that there is no real Political Programme behind it. It lacks the gravitational pull of a true political Big Idea.

Carrying Forward

I promised to say more about the non-radical side of Political Programmes. A new Programme will also contain important content borrowed from the previous one. There will be some *Models*. New Labour shared Thatcherism's respect for market mechanisms and the entrepreneurial approach to wealth-creation. There will be some *Values*. Economic growth has been regarded by all Programmes as desirable (as we hurtle towards ecological disaster, this may change). There will be some *Core Policies*. The welfare reforms of 1945 Socialism were continued by its One Nation Conservative successor, and this continuity was a key part of the new Programme's message. Even themes or characters from *Stories* may be carried forward, though Stories in full tend to be fresh for each Programme. Lloyd George's post-1918 Programme and its successor, Tranquillity, were equally keen to protect the nation from the Villain of Bolshevism. Of course, all content that is carried forward in this way will be remixed and reframed to fit the new culture.

Carrying forward will disappoint the more extreme supporters of the Programme, who will want to reinvent everything, but these hotheads will be overruled.

Undemocratic Programmes may try reinventing everything. In France in 1789, in Russia in 1917, in Germany in 1933, in China in 1949, in Cambodia in 1975, everything was remade, including (in theory) human nature, and woe betide anyone who did not buy into this remaking. Disaster was, and always will be, the inevitable result.

By contrast, democracy, through the rise and fall of Political Programmes, allows a nation's institutions to evolve, adapting to a perpetually changing world roughly in line with popular views and without bloodshed. That is its wonder.

A Political Programme is...

Original

       It is based on genuinely fresh thinking (a Blue Ocean)...

       ...though some old material will be carried forward and remixed

Timely

       It resonates with the spirit of its era (Zeitgeist)

       This gives it Cultural Power

Politically Successful

       It gains a Landslide win, which gives it Political Power

It consists of...

Models

       How the world works: tech, economics, sociology (etc.)

       Human psychology

Values

       Good vs Bad, Right vs Wrong

Stories

       The First (Slaying the Dragon)

- Something of great value...
- ...under dire threat from a malign force
- The Rescue. How the good guys will win.

       The Second (Building a Bright Future)

- The good things that will happen once virtue prevails.

Core Policies

       Radical and substantial

       Prioritized

       'Not for turning'

The Big Idea

       The 'elevator pitch'

       A distillation of all the above into a word, phrase or sentence.

       Much, much more than a Slogan

Science: An Inspiration

In this chapter, I want to look at a big influence on my model. That might seem self-centred, but my aim is to make the model clearer.

The influence comes from the history and philosophy of science, or more specifically, from attempts to model the structure and life-cycle of scientific theories. The two classic texts in this field are Thomas S Kuhn's book *The Structure of Scientific Revolutions* and an essay by philosopher Imre Lakatos called *The Methodology of Scientific Research Programmes*.

Kuhn's book, published in 1962, is best known for having coined the word 'Paradigm', which is now often used for any collection of ideas. Though I hear that word used by some very bright people, I prefer to avoid it, as it has become debased through overuse. A Paradigm is not just any old bundle of ideas, but ideas organized in a particular way, where they are clustered round an unquestioned core vision.

Lakatos, writing a few years later, refined Kuhn's notion. Instead of 'Paradigms', he talked about 'Research Programmes'. His concept was essentially similar, but he added greater depth: he had a much clearer understanding of how these big scientific theories run out of steam and are superseded. I have borrowed Lakatos' term, and talk about 'Political Programmes' rather than 'Political Paradigms'.

Kuhn wrote his book in response to an argument in the philosophy of science about the question, 'How does science progress?'

In the nineteenth century, it was generally believed that science was getting ever better by discovering more and more laws. (Victorian historians like GB Macaulay thought the same about history.) It did this by observing phenomena, hypothesizing laws from these observations, testing these laws by experiment and proving the laws if the experiments worked.

The twentieth-century philosopher Karl Popper disagreed. Annoyed by a rising tide of what he called 'pseudo-scientific' ideas, including psychoanalysis and Marxism, he argued that real science progressed by observing phenomena, hypothesizing laws from these observations, testing these laws by experiment and *dis*proving them if the experiments *didn't* work. He went as far as to say that scientific 'knowledge' wasn't really knowledge at all but a series of 'conjectures' that hadn't been refuted yet.

Popper contrasted this acceptance of fallibility on the part of proper scientists with the behaviour of pseudo-scientists, who, when their theories failed (by making predictions that turned out wrong), devoted their time and energy to finding ever more ingenious ways of explaining the failure away, defending their precious core theories against inconvenient reality (and often launching personal attacks on opponents, for example as 'repressed' or 'bourgeois').

This appeared to be a major step forward, as it cleared up the rules of the game. But Kuhn came along and spoilt things by pointing out that actual science didn't work the way Popper suggested, and could never do so. In actual science, Kuhn said, big overarching theories such as Newtonian mechanics, elements-based chemistry or Darwin's theory of evolution are *not* open to disproof (in anything other than the very long term). They are assumed, with almost the same level of unquestioning acceptance shown by Freudians and Marxists. When anomalies emerge, working scientists do not ditch Newton, the Periodic Table or evolution, but do exactly the same as Popper's pseudo-scientists; they look for ways of squaring the anomaly with their overarching theory. They can do this in various ways:

- by creating new sub-theories
- by patching up existing sub-theories
- by making specific criticisms of whatever experiment or observation(s) had produced the anomaly
- by simply ignoring the anomaly.

The last of these might seem terribly unscientific, but was not uncommon. From the mid-1850s, astronomers had known that the planet Mercury appeared to move in a way that didn't fit the Newtonian model. However, this had not led to any rewriting of the big theory, only to intrigued puzzlement. One day, Newtonians were sure, an explanation would be found. In fact, the observations only came to make sense once Einstein had produced his Newton-transcending General Theory of Relativity in 1915.

'Paradigm' was Kuhn's word for the big intellectual tent within which overarching theories are assumed and where practical, day-to-day scientific work is carried on in their clear, unquestioned light. He called the work that is done within this tent *Normal Science*, as it is what scientists normally do: measuring things, creating and testing new concepts and/or sub-theories, inventing or refining technologies – all using the big theory as an ultimate basis. Normal Science, he argued, does use Popperian trial and error about its sub-theories and technologies. It is prepared to drop them if they don't work. But the beliefs at the heart of the Paradigm remain beyond question.

That point was well taken, but it reignited the old debate. If the big theories are beyond question, how does science progress? Is it just a shouting match between two groups of equally convinced fanatics? The 'geocentric' model of the universe, where all heavenly bodies revolved round the earth, reigned supreme in the classical world and Europe's Middle Ages, but was eventually ditched. How? Why?

This is where Lakatos came in, producing a logical model of Research Programme change. In this, anomalies in a Research Programme begin to build up over time. More and more things happen in ways the big theory says they shouldn't. After a bit of work, these get explained by new sub-theories (Lakatos, who liked long words, called these 'auxiliary hypotheses'). However, the explanations become more and more convoluted and less and less useful. Rather than make interesting new predictions, the new explanations just account for the anomaly (plus a few cases like it). They are simply patching the big theory up. Over time, the Programme becomes full of such patches, like an old bicycle tyre. Lakatos called models in that condition 'degenerating Research Programmes' (and argued that Freudianism and Marxism fell into this category).

Fine, but what causes actual change? Lakatos said that the degenerating Research Programme keeps limping along, however convoluted and clogged with patches it has become, until a better big, overarching model appears. By 'better', he meant a number of things. First, the new overarching model explains the biggest anomalies that have started to bug the old one (or most of these anomalies, anyway). Secondly, it also explains all (or most of) the phenomena that the old model had, once so proudly, explained. Thirdly, it comes armed with new concepts, so offers exciting new avenues for both pure research and technological development. Fourthly, it will stick its neck out make bold new predictions – which start coming true. Fifthly, it has an aesthetic appeal: it is simpler.

Lakatos was keen to point out that the new, better Research Programme doesn't appear fully-fledged in a moment of inspiration. It may start with a flash of inspiration – the apple landing on Isaac Newton's head is the classic example (even if that never actually happened, it's a great story). But it takes time to develop, 'slowly, by a long, preliminary process of trial and error'. Antoine Lavoisier produced his *Traité Élémentaire de Chimie,* which defined and listed the chemical elements, as he understood them at the time, in 1789. Mendeleev's definitive Periodic Table of elements did not appear till eighty years later. Darwin took twenty-five years to finesse his theory of evolution before he went public with it in 1859, and the Research Programme didn't really get its stranglehold on biological thinking till the discovery of the work of Gregor Mendel on heredity in 1900.

During its infancy, the developing Research Programme faces powerful challenges that could overwhelm it. Supporters of the old one will fight back. Darwinism was initially ridiculed by many. "Am I descended from a monkey through my grandmother or my grandfather?" Bishop Samuel Wilberforce asked Darwinist TH Huxley, with a big (and probably annoyingly smug) grin on his face. There will be phenomena that the new theory doesn't explain. The Victorian era's leading physicist, Lord Kelvin, doubted that, given the age of the earth, evolution would have had enough time to come up with humanity. Darwin was genuinely troubled by this, but didn't rip up his ideas. The earth has turned out to be ten times older than Kelvin thought.

The growing Programme ignores criticism, keeping its head down and getting on with gathering evidence, dealing with problems and developing sub-theories and technologies based on the central idea. At the same time, the old one becomes more and more clogged up. Ultimately the new one begins to accelerate past it.

A key moment in this overtaking is a Crucial Experiment. A situation is imagined, where the old theory predicts one outcome and the challenger theory predicts a different one. This situation is then created in a lab (or sought out: astronomers have travelled the world to make crucial observations). The outcome decides between the two Programmes. Galileo's observations of moons orbiting the planet Jupiter are often regarded as the Crucial Experiment that tipped the scales against geocentric astronomy.

After failure in a Crucial Experiment, an old theory which up to that moment was putting up a strong rearguard action will go into rapid and irreversible decline.

Kuhn believed that the new Paradigm used a different language to the old one, and that, as a result, practitioners within the old and the new ones lived in different, irreconcilable conceptual worlds. So 'old Paradigm' stuff was useless. Lakatos disagreed: people in different Research Programmes can and do talk to one another about sub-theories and technology. He also pointed out that no new Programme sweeps away the entire edifice of the old one. He talked instead of new Programmes being 'grafted' onto old ones, the way that, in horticulture, one plant is inserted into the base of another and then grows from it. Much technology and some sub-theories get carried forward. We no longer accept Newtonian mechanics to be *the* explanation of the cosmos or the workings of the sub-atomic world, but we still build skyscrapers and bridges on principles based on it.

21

<u>So what's all this got to do with politics?</u>
This book argues that the history and practice of politics is similar to that of science in a number of major ways.

The Big Idea of a Political Programme is analogous to the big theory at the heart of a scientific Research Programme: Newton's laws, the Periodic Table, Darwinian evolution by natural selection.

- It is simple.

- It informs and inspires everything about the Programme.

- It is not questioned, as to do so would bring the whole edifice crashing down – imagine someone in the current cabinet suggesting we rejoin the European Union or Margaret Thatcher saying we had a lot to learn from Socialist countries.

The Models, Values, Stories and Core Policies of a Political Programme are so closely attached to the Big Idea that they share its unquestionability. Similarly in science, there are bodies of knowledge in Research Programmes, constellated around the Big Idea, whose basic models and principles do not get questioned. The mechanics of materials, organic chemistry, population genetics (and many more disciplines).

Further from these, we enter the realm of *Normal Science*, where falsifiable theories come and go. The same is true in Political Programmes, which can and must come up with lesser policy ideas in response to events. These can be reversed, often are (and probably should be more often). I'll call them 'Normal Politics'.

Scientific Research Programmes *degenerate*. So do Political ones. Some Models start to look false or irrelevant, because they were inadequate to start with (no model of human affairs is perfect) and/or because the world has simply moved on. Values change. Core Policies fail. The Programme no longer aspires to lead events, but starts struggling to keep up with them.

In science and in politics, there is a handover of power from one Programme to another. The paths aren't exactly the same, but there are big similarities.

In science, the battle between two theories is often decided by a *Crucial Experiment*. In politics, I suggest that there are two crucial moments, the 'Body-blow' and 'Waterloo'. I'll explain these terms more fully in the next chapter, but for now... The Body-blow is an event that suddenly reveals the Programme to be inadequate to the changing world and destroys its Cultural Power (this may seem melodramatic, but read on...) 'Waterloo' is when a Programme's Political Power vanishes for good: the Landslide win for its opponent.

In science and politics, it takes two sides to create a crucial moment, a degenerating old Programme and a rising new one. In Lakatos' model of science, if there is *no convincing rival*, the old Programme will just keep bumbling along. For centuries, pre-Copernican astronomers did their best with the old geocentric model. In politics, the same is true. It is a central prediction of this book that only proper Political Programmes, with original Big Ideas and well-formed Models, Values, Stories and Core Policies around them, win Landslides. With one Programme discredited but no real rival on the horizon, politics goes into Drift. The 1970s saw a lack of full-on Programmes, and weak government resulted.

Radical as Scientific Revolutions are, the *change is not all-consuming*. Some concepts, sub-theories and technologies will be grafted from one Research Programme to another. Similarly, new Political Programmes will carry forward some ideas and policies from previous ones.

I must end this section by admitting that the analogy is not perfect. No analogy, in the world of human affairs, is. Science is a search for absolute, eternal truth. Politics is less ambitious: the search for the best solutions for current and looming problems. Science, at its heart, has a static target, politics a moving one.

Politics has a strong emotional element, hence the importance of Cultural Power. Scientific Research Programmes do not require this.

Scientific Research Programmes last much longer than Political Programmes, too. Darwinism is still going strong, but the life-cycle of a UK Political Programme is only about fifteen years, sometimes less. Maybe at some time in the future, a Political Programme will come into being that will have greater longevity – but given the pace of change in the world, this seems unlikely. With the human capacity for corruption, smugness and gaming systems, that seems a good thing. Fifteen (or so)-year political cycles are good for us.

However, the nature and life-cycles of big scientific theories and of Political Programmes have deep similarities. Both science and democracy have been successful due to their mixture of trial-and-error (in Normal Science and Normal Politics), the clarity given by a powerful overarching vision, and the flexibility to allow, over time, change at the profoundest level through clear, crucial deciding events.

In the next section, I shall look at the political life-cycle in greater detail.

Scientific Revolutions...

Thomas Kuhn, The Structure of Scientific Revolutions
Imre Lakatos, The Methodology of Scientific Research Programmes

Research Programmes (Paradigms)

Based on a big, overarching core theory (e.g., Newton, Darwin) which is *not* questioned

'Normal Science' (trial and error) carries on within the Programme

The Programme starts to degenerate

Anomalies start building up

They get explained away, but ever more unconvincingly

Programmes are only changed when a more powerful rival comes along

A Crucial Experiment convinces a critical mass of scientists

Some sub-theories and technologies are carried forward into the new model

...and Political Change

- *The Big Idea* at the heart of a Political Programme is simple and unquestioned
- *The Models, Values, Stories and Core Policies* of a Political Programme are so closely attached to the Big Idea, that they share its unquestionability
- *Normal Politics*: non-core policies will be needed to deal with events beyond the scope of core theory, but can be dropped
- Political Programmes *degenerate* slowly...
- ...but are actually destroyed at *Crucial moments*
- However, they are not fully unseated until a *superior rival*, with its own Models, Values, Core Policies and Big Idea, comes along.
- Some material gets *carried forward* from one Programme to the next.

Rise and Fall:

The Life-Cycle of a Political Programme

Imre Lakatos created a model of how scientific Research Programmes rise and fall. In this section of the book, I would like to do the same for Political Programmes.

<u>In the beginning…</u>
There's a debate about the extent to which great scientific theories are the result of individual or team effort. Arguably their birth is an individual effort: Newton, Lavoisier, Darwin… However, even the notoriously prickly Newton said that he had 'stood on the shoulders of giants' to create his theories.

Similarly, in politics, the inspirational texts behind Political Programmes tend to be the works of inspired individuals. I call these the Programme's *Sacred Texts*.

Most Programmes will have a small *Canon* of these, that lay out basic Models and Values. They are usually speculative, written before a Programme gains momentum. They sow seeds, get people thinking…
At the end of the nineteenth century, the people who would create New Liberalism read the work of Oxford philosopher TH Green. Other Sacred Texts are written later, as a Programme is gathering momentum, summing up the intellectual progress that has been made. LT Hobhouse's *Liberalism* did this for the New Liberals in the twentieth century.

However, not even the most inspirational texts create Programmes on their own. It takes a *team* to do this. In the 1990s, psychologist Kevin Dunbar examined scientists at work in different social settings, and found that the most productive sources of innovation were group discussions, with 'a dozen or so' individuals involved. All participants were talented and able in their own right, but the group setting enabled these bright people to shine even brighter. According to former Columbia Professor Katherine Phillips, diversity within the group is essential: 'informational diversity', diversity of perspectives, among a group that is in other ways homogenous, focused on the same problems and with (largely) shared core beliefs.

In both science and politics, the group needs to be connected to sources of power. The Programme-generating groups that we will meet in the narrative section of this book all contain people with influence in their party. The exception, perhaps, is the anti-EU Bruges Group, which was founded by a student. But he soon got connected individuals on board.

I call such formative collections of individuals *Crucible Groups*. They will end up arguing out all the elements of a Political Programme. Which Models and Values do they share most deeply? What aspects of their Models do they need to investigate more thoroughly? (I remember eager young Thatcherites in 1979 having endless debates about how to measure money supply.) Which Central Stories move them most deeply? Who are the real Villains? Who are the Archetypes? What policies are possible? What policies are best? How, exactly, would these policies be implemented? In what order? Policies must be thought through with particular care, as the Programme will ultimately stand or fall by them. The discussions will bring the Big Idea into ever clearer focus. What is the Programme really all about?

The idea of a unique Crucible Group is no doubt an oversimplification. There may be several. The contemporary political scene is awash with think tanks. But if your ambition is to create a new Political Programme, my advice is to form a Crucible Group as soon as possible.

If the Crucible Group is purely composed of intellectuals, a second group may be necessary once it has done its job. The Programme will need an *Action Group* to get out there and promote the new ideas. This will probably contain the leading thinkers, but also requires:

- A marketing/media expert. Dominic Cummings' understanding of new media was essential to the success of the 2016 Brexit campaign. Cummings was later ditched: being in the Crucible or Action Group doesn't mean a place at the top table, where, in the end, non-party mavericks don't fit.

- Bloggers and other opinion-formers. Ideally, one of these will write a message-spreading Sacred Text for the Programme.

- Doers, organizers, people who 'make things happen'.

- A backer, someone with deep pockets who can fund research, publicity etc.

Early Adopters

How does the Programme develop from its early start? The Big Idea and its intellectual 'planets' begin to spread out from the Crucible Group, as members tell their friends, who in turn tell their friends (and so on). Some of these won't get it, but for others, the new ideas will be a blast of fresh air. "Of course!" Some will become true fans.

These initial fans will be what marketers call 'Early Adopters'. Being an Early Adopter in politics can require courage. The new Programme will probably be unpopular, amid the ranks of the people that will end up supporting it, let alone with the rest of the world. The first Thatcherites were looked on with suspicion within the early 1970s Conservative Party. One member of the Programme's Crucible Group, Keith Joseph, was nicknamed 'the mad monk'. In 2013, a leading Tory – we never found out who – described Brexiters as 'mad, swivel-eyed loons'.

<u>Crossing the (First) Chasm</u>
Keeping the marketing metaphor going, the next group of people to take up a product or technology are called the 'Early Majority'. Unlike Early Adopter fans, the Early Majority are more sceptical. They want to know clearly, in advance, what the product or technology (or, in this case, Programme) will do for them. But they are much more numerous than the Early Adopters. Succeed here, and you are in business.

Silicon Valley guru Geoffrey Moore has pointed out that there is a 'chasm' between these two groups. Many bright tech ideas fall into it, never to reappear. The nerds get it; the herd doesn't. The same can go for bright political ideas.

The Action Group is essential here, skilfully spreading the word beyond the charmed circle of enthusiastic Early Adopters.

The self-reinforcing spiral of both riding and shaping the Zeitgeist is beginning!

As the word spreads, so will the criticisms. But Leaders, founders and fans of a new Programme will take this in their stride. A more insidious type of opposition is when potentially powerful allies within the Programme's home party start saying they will support you *if* you water the Action Plan down in a few ways. These should be resisted – in a friendly manner, of course. If an Aspirant Programme has the Zeitgeist behind it, momentum will soon carry it past the need for such semi-allies. These people will probably join later, suddenly affected by amnesia about their previous objections.

While this is happening, the world is not static. Times are changing, and the current dominant Programme will be struggling ever more to keep up with this. It may well be actively degenerating. People in the Aspirant Programme's home party will sense blood, and be actively looking for the best possible alternative. There will be a moment when a critical mass is reached, when people in the home party suddenly start seeing the new Programme as this alternative.

Leadership

This seems a good moment to discuss Political Programme Leadership. Forests have been felled to create books on leadership, so I don't want to go on too much about this. I would like to make two points.

First, *timing*. The Leader is usually part of the Crucible and/or Action Groups, but some have taken over a Programme once it is underway.

The Programmes of 1906 and 1924 each started off with able Leaders, Henry Campbell-Bannerman and Andrew Bonar Law. However both men's health failed early in their administrations, allowing names who became more famous (Herbert Asquith, Stanley Baldwin) to take – and keep – the reins.

At other times, the first-up leader just isn't good enough. Harold Macmillan was the third Fifties 'One Nation' Conservative PM. His predecessors had been Winston Churchill, who was too old by the time the Programme came to power, and Anthony Eden, who had health issues. After them, Macmillan took command of the Programme and steered it for seven years. Nigel Farage gave the Populist 'Brexit' Nationalism Programme public credibility, but had no parliamentary presence and was too much of a loose cannon to be PM. When real power beckoned, Boris Johnson stepped into the Leader's role.

Such late-arrival Leaders aren't simply jumpers on a bandwagon. They will have been involved in the Programme for a long time, and their loyalty runs deep. Macmillan wrote a proto-manifesto in 1938 for the Programme that he came to lead in 1957. Johnson, despite his apparent hesitation in supporting Brexit in early 2016, had years of journalistic experience of mocking the EU.

Leaders who led Political Programmes from the start include Lloyd George, Clement Attlee, Harold Wilson, Margaret Thatcher and Tony Blair.

Secondly, I can't help commenting on the analogy between Political Programme Leaders and *entrepreneurs*.

Entrepreneurs have a clear, distinct and often contrarian personal vision and a dedication to realizing that vision that can seem irrational to most other people. As they set about that realization, they ruffle feathers – but they also arouse great loyalty among 'their' people, both within their organizations and among their organization's customers. They understand these customers deeply and intuitively. I once suggested a business idea to Jason Porter, founder of Friends Reunited. He thought for a moment then shook his head. 'Our people wouldn't like that,' he said.

Entrepreneurs' intuition extends to their era. In the early 2000s two

31

Harvard academics, Nitin Nohria and Anthony Mayo, looked into the careers of 1,000 American business leaders. Their aim was to find what the most successful ones shared. The answer was not ruthlessness, charisma, hard work or even industry experience. It was attunement to the Zeitgeist.

Another similarity: many entrepreneurs have a 'Foil', someone with a specific skill in an area that he or she lacks but which is essential to the business' success. The entrepreneur usually hogs the public glory but in private listens very carefully to the Foil (who, in turn, is usually happy to remain in the background, exercise their skill and watch their stock options rise in value). Leaders of Political Programmes can have such a person as well – though, as the Foil is a fellow politician, he or she will not be so bashful. Examples? Asquith and Lloyd George. Attlee and Bevin. Wilson and Roy Jenkins. Thatcher and (a rare Foil who was happy to stay in the background) Whitelaw. Blair and Brown. Later, the Foil may turn against the Leader, as happened in the first and last of the above examples.

Political Programme Leaders

Are usually there from the beginning…
> But not always (Macmillan, Johnson)

Are like entrepreneurs
> A distinct vision
> Passionate commitment to that vision
> Intuitive connection to (a large section of) voters
> In tune with the Zeitgeist
> Have a 'Foil'

Gaining Significant Influence

The word is getting out there. The Programme now has growing support, among a wider selection of people than its original fans. The next big step in its march to power is when it gains what I call Significant Influence. This is most obviously gained if a Programme has a Leader in place and that person is elected to a major position. The most common one is that of leader of the entire party, as it was for Attlee, Wilson, Thatcher and Blair. The Programme is now The Party Line, not just one strand of opinion.

This is a great moment. However, it does not guarantee subsequent triumph. Aspirant Political Programmes can get this far, then fail. There is a second chasm it can tumble into, between the 'Early Majority' party activists/loyal voters who have taken the Programme this far, and the wider, more sceptical voting public. The Programmes of left-wing Labour leaders, such as Michael Foot and Jeremy Corbyn, tend to fall into this chasm. The Conservative Party, usually more alert to what voters want, is less prone to getting this wrong.

The First Taste of Actual Power

From Significant Influence, the next step is to Actual Power. This might seem to be the crucial change, but it is not. A First Taste of Power is almost always tenuous.

In a democracy, this can mean being part of a coalition, or being a minority government, or having a tiny majority, or even having a slightly bigger majority but being under a barrage of sustained criticism (the last of these was the case for Thatcherism, whose First Taste of Power came via a majority of 43, but which remained embattled for much of its first term). In undemocratic politics, the revolution is unfinished: Russia's 1917 February Revolution removed the Czar but did not bring the

33

Bolsheviks sole power.

In all cases, the Programme's opponents still have a lot of clout. They fancy their chances and do their damnedest to kill this upstart. Many people still write the new Programme off as a 'flash in the pan'. Its grasp on power, they think, is probationary and will soon slip.

Sometimes they are right. There's a third chasm here. The electorate can take the Aspirant Programme for a test drive but end up handing the keys back to the salesperson. Classic examples are the 1929 Ramsay Macdonald administration, Ted Heath's 1970/4 administration and the Liberal Democrats' 'Orange Book' movement. In all those cases, the Programme got one hand on the lever of power, being the biggest party in the first two examples, membership of a coalition in the third. Rather than stick to their Core Policies and go on to greater things, all of them then made U-turns. Macdonald cut unemployment benefit. Heath did a series of turns. The Lib Dems raised student fees. All those actions can be rationally explained as logical reactions to events, but in all cases the electorate was unforgiving.

By contrast, successful Political Programmes use their First Taste of Power to learn government and turn it into a springboard for greater things. If they have enough momentum, they may leap very quickly over the third chasm. In 1905, the New Liberals were handed their First Taste of Power by their split-riven opponents, who asked them to form a minority government, in the expectation they would do so and then crash. They did so, then called an immediate election, which they won with a Landslide. Nearly a century later, New Labour leapt this third chasm altogether.

Three Chasms

Between 'Early Adopters' and the 'Early Majority'
    It's a totally new movement which never really takes off
    (e.g. Common Wealth and Natural Law Parties)
    or
    It's a movement within an existing major party
    Fans love it – but few others in the party do
    (e.g. 'Keep Left' group in Clement Attlee's government)

Between Significant Influence and a Taste of Actual Power
    The party and loyal voters love it, but wider voters don't
    (E.g. Corbyn, 2019)

One Hand on Power – but that slips
    Voters lose confidence/conviction. The 'test drive' fails
    (E.g. 'Orange Book' Liberals, 2015)

The Great Endorsement: The Landslide

What a true Political Programme needs, and gets, is a full-throated roar of public approval, a Great Endorsement. The Great Endorsement is the 'Political Success' in my definition of what a Political Programme is. That is what separates it from the Aspirants that end up just as clever sets of ideas or interesting (to the political historian) movements. These are the Landslide election wins: the Liberals in 1906, Lloyd George in 1918, the Conservatives in 1924, Labour in 1945, the Conservatives in 1955, Labour in 1966, the Conservatives in 1983, Labour in 1997, the Conservatives in 2019.

What constitutes a proper Landslide? If asked to pin down a precise figure, I would say 60 seats or more. 100 is the ideal: there's something special about the 'ton', like a century in cricket. However, (to keep the cricket analogy going) 60 in a low-scoring game can be a match-winning innings. In practice, election results tend to be either close or convincing, with little ground in between. Yes, there *are* 'in between' cases. Margaret Thatcher's 43-seat majority in 1979 was nice (for her), but many people still thought her position precarious. They didn't think this after her 144-seat win in 1983. Ted Heath's 30-seat win in 1970 was insufficient: he was unable to enact one half of his Core Policies and crashed out of office at the next election.

Looking further back, Conservative Andrew Bonar Law won a 74-seat majority in 1922, taking power from the Liberals. However, various factors, including his own poor health, soon undermined that majority. The new leader, Stanley Baldwin, was forced to go to the country again the very next year – and lost. Had he fallen into the third chasm? If so, he soon clambered out of it. Ten months later, in October 1924, a third election occurred, and this time Baldwin won by a thumping 210 seats. This was a Great Endorsement for him, which enabled his Programme to run for a full term and then, in the guise of a National Government, to run the country (with a short intermission 1929 – 31) until 1940.

Only with a Great Endorsement does a Programme have the space and time to truly implement its Core Policies. Jim Prior's view that the best governments have small majorities, thus keeping a 'balance of power', is 100% wrong. It is only when given Great Endorsements that administrations can really bring about the deep and difficult changes that they – and the large number of citizens who voted for them – regard as necessary to keep the nation's institutions up to speed with a fast-changing world.

The phrase 'The Will of the People' comes into its own at this moment. Small wins are more a sign that the People aren't really sure, but after a Great Endorsement, there is certainty. The 2016 Brexit referendum, with its relatively close result, was arguably not an expression of such a clear-cut will. The 80-seat win by the hard-Brexit-supporting Conservatives in December 2019 was.

In undemocratic politics, the Great Endorsement is not so much a roar of public approval as the completed seizure of the instruments of government, after which roars of public approval can be orchestrated. In the Russian example, this is probably the October revolution, though one could argue that the Soviets only had total power with the fall of Vladivostok in October 1922. In Germany, Hitler won the March 1933 election but did not gain an overall majority. He then quickly tightened his grip on power; by September of that year, Germany was a one-party state.

Pomp

After a Landslide, the Programme has its hands on the levers of Political Power firmly and (at least for five, or probably ten, years) immovably. It has massive Cultural Power: many people 'get' it, and doubters are seen as losers or dinosaurs. The Programme enters the phase of its *Pomp*.

Time to fully realize the Action Plan. This is the time of *Big Wins,* of radical and long-lasting changes. Lloyd George's People's Budget. The National Insurance and NHS Acts of 1946. Roy Jenkins' social liberalization. Margaret Thatcher's privatization programme. Johnson's hard Brexit.

Sometimes, these wins will be gained in the teeth of entrenched institutions which were regarded as unassailable by previous

37

Programmes. These institutions have a strong sense of entitlement, and don't give up without a fight. Cue the Programme's *Big Battles*. Asquith and Lloyd George versus the House of Lords. Nye Bevan versus the British Medical Association. Thatcher versus the trade unions (especially the National Union of Mineworkers). But the Great Endorsement means that these bitter, existential battles can be fought and won. That is exactly what a Landslide is for.

In parliament, the opposition benches will be much thinner and in disarray. The government ones will not only be more crowded but filled with new faces: daughters and sons of the new Programme, with an unquestioning loyalty to it, a sense of destiny and a suspicion of whatever went before, in their own party as well as the opposition. Wise Programme Leaders will keep a few old, big-hitting rivals on the front bench, to head off factionalism and because these individuals have genuine ability. But there will be long-serving Programme loyalists who have paid their dues, having been regarded for many years with suspicion by the party's old guard, who now expect cabinet posts. It will be payback time.

An unattractive *Triumphalism* can emerge, a hubristic 'rubbing the old enemy's face in it'. "We are the masters now," said 1945 Socialist Hartley Shawcross in 1946. Little was done to support mining communities after crushing of the 1984/5 strike. The Johnson government initially refused to grant full diplomatic status to the EU ambassador in London. Out come the negative catchphrases, spoken with suitably playground contempt. 1945 Socialists heaped scorn on 'appeasers'. Wilsonite modernizers derided 'grouse-moor' aristocrats. Brexiters taunted 'remoaners'.

Around the time of its Great Endorsement, the new Programme can enjoy an extra-special moment of triumph, a *Crowning Glory*. This is a great public event which shows how in tune the Programme is with the spirit of its age. For 'One Nation' Conservatism, this was Coronation Day in 1953, when the radiant young queen drove past cheering crowds (it was Britain, so she did so through pouring rain) and it was announced *on the same day* that a British expedition had climbed Mount Everest. For Harold Wilson and Roy Jenkins' Programme of modernization, it was England's World Cup victory in 1966. Fate seems to be shouting a great big 'Yes!' to the Programme.

I say, 'around the time', as the Crowning Glory may happen shortly *before* the Great Endorsement. Remember that Political Programmes ride the Zeitgeist, and ever since the First Taste of Power, the momentum of that Zeitgeist has been flowing strongly in the Programme's direction (if it is to become a real Programme, not just another Aspirant), so the exact timing isn't important. The Coronation/Everest was half way between Fifties Conservatism's First Taste and its Great Endorsement, but it was still a massive affirmation of the Programme and what it stood for.

Attempts to manufacture Crowning Glories fail. The 1951 Festival of Britain was supposed to celebrate the culture of Attlee's very British Socialism, but by the time it started, the Programme was staggering towards political defeat. The Millennium Dome was supposed to be a Crowning Glory for Blairism. The £120 million 'Unboxed' festival, informally known as the 'Festival of Brexit', has only been saved from being an embarrassment because hardly anyone knows it is happening. Crowning Glories are radiant and magical *beyond* their planned intentions, which is what makes them special.

As well as these one-off moments, there should be a wider *Cultural Endorsement*. The culture around the new Programme, which shares its

Models and Values and maybe even tells its Stories, was growing before the political Great Endorsement. After that, it will bloom even more: ebullient, unchained, in charge.

Archetypes will bask in the new culture, which is especially about and for them. Leaders, in particular, will fit the new culture like a glove. Stanley Baldwin was an English gentleman; he didn't have to pretend to be. Margaret Thatcher aspired. Tony Blair was young, metropolitan, internationalist.

Cultural Endorsements aren't party political, however. A few artists will come out in formal support for the new Programme – often rather ineptly: Kenny Everett's 1983 advice to Young Conservatives to 'bomb Russia' didn't do Thatcherism or his own image any good. Other creators may be jollied along to events at Number Ten, where they are photographed next to politicians trying to appear casual and where everyone looks rather sheepish. But the true, profound endorsement that I am talking about is never as obvious as that. Culture and politics find themselves marching jubilantly side by side, but not in lockstep.

Totalitarian Political Programmes will pretend to have such Endorsements and churn out formulaic ones. 'People's artists' will make wooden statements about how their work echoes the Thought of the Glorious Leader. In democracies (and especially in Britain) we are deeply suspicious of anything that looks like that. As with the Crowning Glory, the independence of Cultural Endorsements makes them all the more welcome to the Programme, as an affirmation that it really is in tune with a powerful national mood.

Some culture will also be inspired that is a *Counterblast* to the Programme. The 1930s seethed with writers wanting to disturb Baldwinian

Tranquillity. Evelyn Waugh's novels from *Brideshead Revisited* onwards were pot-shots at 1945 Socialism. The Angry Young Men from the mid-1950s were angry at Conservative Britain (bizarrely, many of them turned into even angrier supporters of Conservatism when the national mood changed). Many writers and artists have expressed their dislike of Brexit.

The response from the Programme to Counterblasts is usually disdain. The current Programme has taken this to extremes, actively demonizing the Counterblast and launching a US-style Culture War. By contrast, Harold Macmillan faced the music and went to a performance of the satirical Counterblast revue *Beyond the Fringe* in October 1961. He is, surely, to be admired for this.

Counterblasts may be energetic and powerful, but they are still haunted by the Programme. Hatred of Thatcherism was at the heart of 1980s Counterblast literature. The culture that underpins a new Programme is less reactive. It has found a new way to experience and celebrate life, to which the old Programme is not so much 'the enemy' as an irrelevance. The new Programme swims in a cultural Blue Ocean as well as a political one.

Great Escapes
Early in its Pomp, the new administration can get away with major policy errors. That is due to their Cultural Power. Their opponents may fume and history may judge harshly, but a crucial mass of the public is still so relieved to have an administration that sees things their way – unlike the last lot – that they will forgive or find someone else to blame. The party may have to sacrifice a bigshot or two, but, despite the errors, the polls do not change radically. The Programme marches on. It is too early for real, soul-destroying failure. I call such unpunished errors *Great Escapes* (cue that music...)

41

Great Escapes will add to that secretly-held belief among fans that the Programme will last not just for a parliamentary term or two but much, much longer. The ideas behind the Programme are, after all, The Truth… This is taken to ludicrous extents by totalitarian regimes. Hitler hoped his Reich would last a thousand years. The slogan 'Long Live the Chinese Communist Party!' (*Zhongguo Gongchandang wansui!*) literally wills it to last ten thousand. But even in democratic Programmes, in their Pomp the most fanatical supporters secretly believe they have cracked the secret of good government, just as, when we were teenagers, at least a part of us thought we were immortal.

In reality, the Pomp of a Programme usually lasts about five years. Some are lucky enough to ride the wave for longer; others don't get as much.

The First Big Failure

The Programme in its Pomp appears to be flowing along, conquering all. It has had Great Escapes. Maybe a few bits of Normal Politics turned out to have unexpectedly negative consequences, but Normal Politics can be reversed. But at some point, the Programme will hit its *First Big Failure*. This is an event which wasn't in its playbook, and it does not deal with it at all well. Unlike the Great Escape(s), this time the public (or a significant chunk of it, anyway) is not impressed. Poll ratings fall. A chilling blast of doubt blows into the previously sealed chamber of power.

A classic example is the Iraq War of March/April 2003. In early 2002, the New Labour Programme had massive poll leads, but these leached away as it became ever clearer that Blair was throwing his lot in with President Bush. Tory leads start appearing in the polls in mid-2003, as we realized that the outcome of the conflict was not a quick victory but a quagmire.

However, the First Big Failure is wounding but not fatal. As with Iraq, it may be in foreign policy, which will upset better-informed voters but matter less to others. Many people still feel the Programme in their hearts, and the failure can be explained away. After a while, the poll ratings recover some of their lost ground – but only some. After Iraq, Labour recovered enough to win the 2005 election, albeit with a reduced majority and a poor 35% of the vote.

The Slow Strangler

Political Programmes face forces that eventually drag them down. The most remorseless of these is what I call the *Slow Strangler*. This is a problem that comes up again and again (and again and again), but which the Programme seems helpless to solve. The Programme wasn't designed to address issues like it, and doesn't have the tools in its armoury to do so. The problem is conceptual as well as practical: this isn't just the lack of a tool but a complete inability to comprehend that such a tool might exist, let alone actually be used. This inability is built into the Programme's Worldview. That proud boast at the start, that the new Programme had The Answer – Mrs Thatcher's version was "There is no alternative!" – turns into a bleat of helplessness: "But there isn't anything else we can do!"

There are alternatives, of course – but the existing Programme and its adherents are incapable of seeing them. When a new Programme takes power, it can release the grip of the old Slow Strangler with one slash of an Alexandrian sword, as it has different Models, Values, Stories and Core Policies.

The most painful examples of Slow Stranglers? 'Tranquil' Stanley Baldwin's failure to understand Hitler and Mussolini. Rationing, which slowly strangled 1945 Socialism. Austerity, which did the same for New

Labour and the Coalition that followed it.

Programmes in real difficulty can have more than one of these.

The Big Split

This is another insidious eroder of Political Programmes. Major political parties are uneasy coalitions of groups with very different backgrounds and issues. One of the great achievements of a Political Programme is to unite these usually warring tribes – for a while, anyway. But over time, these differing loyalties start to tell. The Liberal Party was ripped apart by the split between Asquith and Lloyd George (it has yet to recover). In the last days of 1945 Socialism, a large chunk of MPs broke off and supported the policy ideas of Nye Bevan, who had resigned from the government. After the departure of Margaret Thatcher, the Conservative Party split over Europe, her normally mild-mannered successor John Major being driven to refer to his Eurosceptic opponents as 'bastards'.

With a seriously split party, policy decisions become more about trying to appease the splinter group than about the needs of the country or any remaining commitment to the old Worldview or Core Policies. Voters look at the party and wonder who is really in charge.

The Body-blow

The Slow Stranglers and the Big Split are hard at work undermining the Programme, but what breaks it for good – bang! – is a particularly destructive event, or set of closely related events, that I call the Body-blow.

This kicks away a key prop of the Programme. After it, the Programme never gets its energy back again, try as it might. Outside the once-charmed circle of the Programme's creators and fans, its once-impressive rhetoric starts to feel shrill and irrelevant. Its assumptions are increasingly questioned, even within the Programme's own party. Who says it has to be this way? Its coded insults, which once sent a frisson of fear down the spines of its opponents, now elicit yawns or groans. Just as the Programme once rose via a seemingly unstoppable self-reinforcing spiral of its own enthusiasm and a new Zeitgeist, it is now disappearing into an equally relentless spiral in the opposite direction. Just as it helped create the upward cultural/political spiral, it now helps create the downward one. The Profumo affair in 1963 didn't single-handedly destroy the nation's trust in the old class system that had sustained the Fifties Conservative Programme, but it had a major role in that change.

This can happen surprisingly fast. An impressive-looking façade can suddenly crack, just as a once-flourishing species can suddenly die out in the 'punctuated evolution' model.

Body-blows can come from outside ('exogenous shocks', in the language of economists and systems theorists). Examples? The emerging nature of the First World War in late 1914, as the front line turned into 475 miles of trenches, to which idealistic New Liberalism had no answer. New Labour and the 2008 financial crash (which was partially the fault of the Programme, with its anti-regulation approach, but also driven by events in the USA).

Or they can be self-inflicted. The recent Truss/Kwarteng fiasco was willed on the Conservative Party by itself. Self-infliction can also take the form of a U-turn on a Core Policy, which is essentially an admission that the administration has no real direction any more. A classic example: the 1921/2 'Axe' taken by Eric Geddes to Lloyd George's second Programme, when socially beneficial government expenditure was slashed in response to a financial crisis – a radical change of direction that ripped the Liberalism out of the Welshman's post-war administration.

It might seem a little 'over the top', but most Programmes are destroyed by Body-blows – see Appendix E at the end of this book. Not every administration ends like this, however. That of Clement Attlee suffered a more attritional fate, with a series of unpleasant but not fatal blows, a Big Split and a particularly malevolent Strangler in the form of unending rationing. Historians Robert Crowcroft and Kevin Theakston described its demise as 'more a whimper than a bang'. This was an exception, however.

Limping Along

A Political Programme, post Body-blow, is a sorry sight. It no longer seeks to lead events, but struggles to keep up with them. It can try and hide this by producing catchy policies, created seemingly out of nowhere, that have little to do with the original Programme (someone in Party HQ just thought the public might like them). Some of these ideas work, others are ignored, others generate gleeful sarcasm. John Major's National Lottery fell into the first category, his Citizen's Charter the second, his Cones Hotline the third.

A Body-blow is a one-off event (or a series of linked such events, such as the 1978/9 Winter of Discontent): the Big Splits and Slow Stranglers that were assailing the Programme beforehand will still be at work – but after the Body-blow they will get more vicious, as their prey is now much, much weaker. One is reminded of wounded wildebeest in nature documentaries who start lagging behind the pack then get separated from it. The lions start licking their lips…

Why do some Political Programmes limp along for a long time while others vanish mercifully quickly?

One reason is simply the electoral cycle. The once-mighty Thatcherite Programme suffered its Body-blow soon after a (narrow) election victory, which left it the best part of five years of apparent executive power but with no real energy.

But also remember Lakatos' model of science, where a degenerating Research Programme continues until something better becomes available (he carefully set out his criteria for 'better'). The same is true in politics. Here, 'better' means a Programme with a new set of Models, Values, Stories and Core Policies; with a Big Idea with solutions to the old one's Slow Strangler(s); with vitality and, above all, with that magic admixture of Timeliness, of resonating with an emerging Zeitgeist.

Sometimes, such a Programme is waiting in the wings, already a-crest a rising Zeitgeist. In 1964. the Wilson/Jenkins 'White Heat' Programme was in position, eager to pounce on dying Fifties Conservatism. At other times, when one Programme is clearly broken but there's no convincing, passion-arousing one to replace it, politics can go into periods of Drift. This happened in the mid/late 2010s, when the existing parties were all in turmoil and a new Programme, Populist 'Brexit' Nationalism, was gathering strength but was not yet ready for power. It happened in the 1970s from the Heath U-turns in 1971/2 to the rise of Thatcherism. It happened in the 1990s from Black Wednesday to the rise of New Labour. It is my contention that this is also happening now, but more on this later.

During periods of Drift, the broken Programme may appear to recover a bit – its poll ratings might stop looking utterly dreadful. But this rarely lasts long (in the stock market, people talk about a 'dead cat bounce', when a falling, 'bear' market makes a brief rally). Once voters get a whiff of an alternative, the polls plummet again. Don't buy a dead cat. The game is over.

Why does Drift happen? Maybe the Zeitgeist itself is not quite ready for change. Or the proponents of an appropriate Programme are still too hesitant, or too 'fringe'. Or maybe both.

Whatever the reason, it is time for a creative, entrepreneurial Leader and their team to initiate that upward, self-reinforcing spiral of their active promotion of a new spirit and that spirit's as yet unrealized potential for momentum.

Replacement Leaders

At some point in a Programme's downward spiral, the Leader will usually go – their deposition often accompanied by mutterings about 'treachery' from Programme diehards. Sometimes, as was the case with Thatcherism, they will have been deposed shortly before the Body-blow. At other times, he or she will linger on past it: Harold Macmillan survived the Profumo Affair – just.

A *Replacement Leader* will take over. They will be believers in the Programme, but without the original Leader's messianism.

They have genuine ability. Thatcher's Replacement, John Major was intelligent, fair-minded and, according to people who knew him personally, very witty. His pronouncements since leaving office have been embarrassingly (for his successors) statesmanlike. Gordon Brown went even better: he was probably responsible for saving the UK's, and maybe even the world's, financial system. Try doing that, Tony! They seem to be nicer people than the Leaders they have replaced, too. More

48

nuanced. Less egotistical. There is usually an uptick of voter pleasure at the departure of the old Leader: that tone of voice or that grin had really begun to grate! But…

…Replacement Leaders hardly ever win elections. Arthur Balfour, Alec Douglas-Home, Jim Callaghan and Gordon Brown all failed in this most essential of political tasks. Only Major has had that honour – something he should be extremely proud of.

In the end, the Replacement Leader's 'Political Programme Lite' is not enough. The times, they are a-changin', and they require a new Big Idea and all that goes with it.

In Autocracies

In non-democratic situations, rather than limp along, fatally damaged Political Programmes can respond to their failures by *Clamping Down*, ramping up the rhetoric and the violence. In pure survival terms, this can be a hugely effective strategy. In 2021 we saw the dictatorships in Belarus and Myanmar applying it with dismal success. In both those countries, the tyrants were protected by global powers, so the rest of the world was unable to intervene.

This is, of course, a disaster, for any dissenters but also for the rest of the population, who are being imprisoned in a cultural and political cul-de-sac. The nation can no longer change its institutions to keep up with change in the world out there. Lobsters, apparently, shed their shells a number of times as they grow. The clamping-down dictatorship becomes like such a creature that, for some reason, is unable to do this, and instead becomes trapped in the smallness and increasing irrelevance of its Worldview. Anyone who visited East Germany in the 1970s or 1980s, and saw (and heard and smelt) Trabant cars chugging down potholed streets past half-empty shops, will understand.

Palace Revolutions

However, sometimes a dictatorship can reinvent itself, or at least a part of itself. The Communist Party managed to do this in China and Vietnam. Mysterious leadership struggles behind firmly closed doors can produce sudden changes of leadership and direction: *Palace Revolutions*. Maybe the best that the people on the streets of Minsk or Yangon can hope for is one of these, though given current geopolitics, this looks tragically unlikely.

Palace Revolutions can also happen in democracies, especially during wartime, when the ballot box isn't a viable option. In the second half of 2019 we saw a rare event, a peacetime Westminster Palace Revolution. Boris Johnson wasn't just a new leader for the Conservative Party; his arrival marked its adoption of a totally new Political Programme, Populist 'Brexit' Nationalism.

Palace Revolutions are always cruel. We never hear about the people marched out of the Kremlin or Zhongnanhai, but we did see the Tory party expel some of its most able members, such as Kenneth Clarke, David Gauke, Justine Greening, Oliver Letwin and Rory Stewart, because they would not sing from the new songsheet. Other rising stars such as Anna Soubry and Heidi Allen quit of their own volition, knowing they no longer belonged. When a new Programme gains a Landslide endorsement at the ballot box, it does not have to be so ruthless. Able doubters can be kept in place: Margaret Thatcher kept 'wets' in her cabinet throughout the 1980s. Programmes installed by Palace Revolutions are more insecure and seem to need a radical purge.

The result of this will be a much-diminished pool of talent in the governing party. This is a danger for peacetime Palace Revolutionaries. By contrast, when such revolutions happen in wartime, as they did in the UK in 1916 and 1940, there is an expanded pool as the parties come together to form the new administration. In 1940, Conservative appeasers were banished but Churchill had the Labour and Liberal parties to draw on.

Journey's End

A democratic Programme's demise can be mapped in a mirror image to its rival's rise. When a rival Programme gets one hand on the levers of power, that is the moment of the old Programme's *Dethronement*. It no longer has a monopoly of power. When the rival grabs all the levers with its Landslide endorsement, the old Programme has met its *Waterloo*.

Routed now, the old Programme enters its final phase, of *Dissolution*. There will be no sniff of power for the now-defunct Programme's party for at least five years, probably more. No wonder: the spirit of the age now looks back on the Programme's Pomp with the kind of embarrassment people feel after they have drunk too much and misbehaved at a social event. Did our leaders really say that? Did we really think that policy would work? The Programme's party (which was always bigger than the Programme, however much it got into line during the Pomp) may start tearing itself apart. "You lot got us into this mess!" cry people who never really liked the Programme anyway but who put up with it because it promised office. Pundits start asking, "Will the x Party ever hold power again?" (Diehards, of course, will have none of this. The Old King – or Queen – is still sleeping in their cave, and one day will rise again to save the nation. One day…)

This is a Time of Ashes for the party. However, Political Programmes are mortal, like individuals, but the parties that host them are like dynasties. They (except the Liberals after 1922) will reinvent themselves. What can the opposition do during its Time of Ashes? It must face up to its situation. Times have changed; the electorate has cast it into the wilderness, and it won't be coming back any time soon.

There is opposition to be carried on – the unglamorous business of scrutinizing the government's actions, of speaking truth to power, of pointing out inconsistencies, moral failings and the consequences of unwise policies. There will be parliamentary committees with a role in policy formation. MPs still have the ongoing duties of looking after constituents and, where legitimate, their interests. All this can be done with thoroughness and pride, and, if individual MPs are up to it, wit. It is the basic job of a Pomp opposition, and carrying it out diligently is important and honourable.

The party needs to end its post-Dissolution bickering. I have my doubts about Sir Kier Starmer as the active, charismatic leader of a new Political Programme, but he has done a great job regrounding Labour.

It can overhaul party admin. David Willetts' *After the Landslide* shows how the Conservatives did this after the Waterloos of 1906 and 1945.

Above all, the opposition to a Programme in its Pomp must wait. Somewhere in the party's midst, ambitious and originally-minded individuals will be getting angry in a new way. Some will get together and start working to clarify their Models, Values and Stories and to create a new Action Plan (which might seem crazy or disloyal or overidealistic to most of their colleagues). If a Pomp opposition leader can encourage the creators of such a Programme, while not really sharing their vision and even coming to realize that they will, at some time, supplant him or her – now, that is mastery.

Coda

As the authors of the *I Ching* understood, the only immutable fact is that of change: social, intellectual, cultural, economic, geographic, technological, ecological.

Eras and their spirits are how we adapt to this perpetual change. They change unevenly because reality is infinitely complex but our ways of looking it are not. We can only lurch from one hopefully-best-as-possible oversimplification to another. In the journey towards absolute truth called science, this happens via Research Programmes. In the much more uncertain world of politics it is via Political Programmes. Political Programmes' Landslides give them time to make (usually) necessary, difficult, substantial changes, especially (but not exclusively) those that upset entrenched interest groups. But even at their most impressive, Political Programmes are only ever based on partial understanding and are doomed to ever-increasing imperfection. Even at the instant of their Great Endorsement, the world out there is already moving on.

Towards what? Nobody knows. The 19th century philosopher Hegel argued that the trial-and-error process of human attempts to model reality was inching towards absolute truth, slowly squeezing out error. But in politics, the opposite seems to be true. Reality keeps changing, and our main job is to try and keep up with it. Political Programmes are best-possible attempts to do so, intellectually and practically, at given historical moments. Hence my comparison between the most influential politicians and entrepreneurs. In an inevitably uncertain world, the best politics is a truly creative activity.

The Life-Cycle of a Political Programme

In the Beginning…
    Sacred Texts (= Canon)
    The Crucible Group
    The Action Group
    The Leader
        May be replaced later if not PM material

Crossing the First Chasm
    Enthusiasm builds outside the 'charmed circle'

Gaining Significant Influence
    (Usually) The Programme Leader takes control of their party

The First Taste of Power
    Actual government (or a role in it)

The Great Endorsement
    The Landslide!

Pomp
    Crowning Glory
        (may precede the Great Endorsement)
    Cultural Endorsement and Counterblasts
    Big Battles
    Big Wins
    Great Escapes
    Triumphalism

The First Big Failure – a wound

Slow Stranglers
> Problems that the Programme is incapable of grasping

The Big Split

The Body-blow
> A major event that destroys the credibility of the Programme
> (See Appendix E for examples)

Limping Along
> If no alternative Programme ready for power
> Usually under a Replacement Leader

Dethronement
> Rival Programme gets provisional hold on power

Waterloo
> Rival Programme gains Great Endorsement

Dissolution
> The Programme, now powerless, rips itself apart
> 'Time of Ashes' for the host political party
> Time to reground, reform, reinvent

In a non-democratic system, there's a similar access to, not a Great Endorsement but a Completed Seizure of Power. Cultural Counterblasts, of course, are soon silenced. Once things start to go wrong, there is…
> Clamping Down
> Ramping up the Rhetoric and the Violence
> Stagnation / Increasing Irrelevance

The Model in Action:
1900 to the Present Day

I'd like to show the life-cycle model I've outlined above at work, in greater detail.

I believe there have been ten proper Political Programmes in British politics since the start of the twentieth century (or eleven if one counts the Marquess of Salisbury's, which was dominant when that century began). The Programmes are:

- New Liberalism

- The Knock-Out Blow (Lloyd George 1.0)

- A Fit Country for Heroes (Lloyd George 2.0)

- Tranquillity (Inter-war Conservatism)

- 1945 Socialism (which actually began in 1940 – I'll explain later)

- Fifties 'One Nation' Conservatism

- 'White Heat' Modernization

- Thatcherism

- New Labour

- Populist 'Brexit' Nationalism

The National Governments from 1931 to 1940 were essentially continuations of the Tranquillity Programme.

Even taking that into account, this list doesn't quite fill out the entire period from 1900 to now, as there have been periods of Drift. The 1920s saw two brief attempts at government by the then-new Labour Party, but those were both Aspirant Political Programmes that failed to achieve a Landslide. The 1970s were a time when both major UK parties attempted to create Political Programmes but failed. The same can be said of the 2010s.

The model I present in this book could be extended beyond Westminster. The rise of Scottish or Welsh Nationalism in their home nations would be a fascinating study. The USA has seen some classic Political Programmes: Theodore Roosevelt's 'Square Deal', FDR's 'New Deal', Lyndon Johnson's 'Great Society'.

I could go back further, too – but the world of Victorian politics is so distant from our own, with its tiny electorates and shifting cabals of aristocrats. Yet even there, there were moments when Big Ideas arose and were eagerly endorsed by those individuals allowed to vote. Such moments were:

- The election of 1831, where the Whig Earl Grey (after whom the tea was named) won a Landslide for his promise to enact the Great Reform Bill, which he did in 1832
- Sir Robert Peel's victory ten years later, for his remade Conservative Party that accepted reform and promised to roll back protectionism, which it did, after much strife, in 1846
- Gladstone's first win in 1868, for the Liberals (the successors to the Whigs) and their agenda of reforming a range of outdated national institutions
- Disraeli's populist Conservative victory in 1874
- The Marquess of Salisbury's 153-seat majority in 1895

The last of these was the dominant Programme when the twentieth century began. It was Victorian to its handmade leather boots. The Marquess, a diffident man with a splendidly late-Victorian bushy beard, was a devout Anglican, deeply distrustful of most attempts by fallible human beings to do anything new. In his view, reforms at home simply jeopardized an economic, ecclesiastical, moral and political system that had made Britain the richest and most powerful nation on earth. Abroad? The best policy was 'to drift lazily downstream'. His strongest active view was vehement opposition to Home Rule for Ireland.

The Programme had its Crowning Glory with Queen Victoria's diamond Jubilee celebrations in 1897. A loud Counterblast to its formal, correct culture came from the dreamy, contrarian, decadent world of Oscar Wilde and Aubrey Beardsley.

After the death of his wife in 1899, Salisbury became ill himself. In 1902 handed over the reins to his Programme's Replacement Leader, his nephew Arthur Balfour.

Like Clement Attlee's '1945 Socialism', Salisbury's Programme never suffered a single, fatal Body-blow. Instead, it was slowly pulled apart by a Big Split, between advocates of Free Trade and those who wanted to turn the Empire into a trading bloc surrounded by import tariffs ('Imperial Preference'). This became ever more vicious from 1903 onwards, and led to Balfour's resignation in 1905.

New Liberalism, 1905 - 1916

New Liberals rejected the old Gladstonian Liberal insistence on *laissez-faire*. At the same time, they kept their distance from Socialist thinkers, who, they considered, played down the role of the individual (politically, however, they were happy to form alliances with the rising Labour Party).

A Sacred Text for the Programme was Oxford philosopher TH Green's uninspiring-sounding *Lecture on Liberal Legislation and Freedom of Contract*, given in 1881. The piece went way beyond this brief, and set out a Model of the Liberal state. For Green, the irreconcilable clash between state and individual, a notion at the heart of Victorian Liberalism, was an illusion. Rather than threatening the freedom of the individual, the state had the capacity to *enable* the individual by combating darker, more insidious enemies of freedom: appalling housing, overlong working hours in unsafe factories, lack of education. By fighting these, a Liberal state would create the circumstances in which every individual was free (in Green's words) 'to make the best of themselves': to flourish spiritually, emotionally and intellectually as well as economically.

Green's psychological Model of 'making the best' was linked to an obscure concept of 'eternal consciousness', but his vision works perfectly well without this (as long as one takes a reasonably optimistic view of human nature). It is, in fact, oddly contemporary, chiming with humanistic psychology. Substitute 'eternal consciousness' with Maslow's Hierarchy of Needs, add talk about 'empowerment' – and we have a very modern approach.

Two more Sacred Texts were the surveys which came out around the turn of the century, and which did away with the old Gladstonian Liberal (and existing Conservative) Model of society as a place where anyone could better their lives if they worked hard and avoided obvious traps like alcohol – a view that implied that there was no point in the state creating freedom-denying and expensive institutions to give helping hands.

Charles Booth's *Life and Labour of the People of London* showed that 35% of London's population lived in extreme poverty. It did so in great detail, mapping the city and showing the levels of income on each street. In many areas, bright red shows the well-to-do living along the great arterial roads, but a few streets behind are squares of black, the homes of the desperately poor.

Seebohm Rowntree's *Poverty, A Study of Town Life*, published in 1901, took the story further. Researching in York, he found that about a quarter of the city's population were in poverty. But his core finding was that half of these families had a full-time wage earner who was paid so badly that the family couldn't get by. Another quarter of them suffered from the wage-earner being sick or having died. These people – together nearly 20% of the city's population – were not feckless, anti-social or alcoholics. They were doing the best they could, playing by the rules, but still did not have an adequate income 'to enable families to secure the necessities of a healthy life'.

Needless to say, both these surveys were criticized by political opponents as being flawed, biased or anecdotal, but to any objective reader at the time, they were thorough and horrifying. A rising young Conservative MP called Winston Churchill said that reading Rowntree's report 'fairly made my hair stand on end'. The year after he made this comment, he crossed the floor of the House of Commons and joined the Liberals.

The Crucible Group for New Liberalism had formed back in the 1890s. It was called the Rainbow Circle and took its name from the tavern on Fleet Street where it held its first meetings. Leading New Liberal thinkers such as LT Hobhouse, JA Hobson, RB Haldane, Charles Trevelyan and Herbert Samuel attended, along with figures from the emerging Labour movement, including future PM Ramsay Macdonald. Hobhouse would subsequently write a 'summing up' Sacred Text for the Programme, *Liberalism*, published in 1911.

New Liberalism arguably acquired Significant Influence when Henry Campbell-Bannerman was elected party leader in February 1899. However, 'CB', as he was known, was regarded by many as a placeholder for a younger rising star in the party, HH Asquith. It took CB time to come into his own as a Leader. A speech against the conduct of the Boer War in June 1901, where he condemned the 'methods of barbarism' used by the British Army (these included scorched earth policies and concentration camps), made everyone sit up and take notice of this previously quiet Scot – the moment, perhaps, of his real acquisition of influence.

The Programme had had its First Taste of Power in December 1905, when Balfour resigned. King Edward VII asked CB to form a minority government. The Tories believed that it would be a disaster, and that they would soon be back in power (an existing Political Programme's standard reaction to an opponent's First Taste of Power).

The Liberals immediately called an election, to be held at the beginning of 1906. They proudly announced a list of Core Policies. Free Trade and Home Rule for Ireland were carried forward from Gladstonian

Liberalism, but their new Big Idea was domestic. In Germany, Chancellor Bismarck had introduced a basic Welfare State in the 1880s: old-age pensions, unemployment insurance, health insurance, and free school meals. The New Liberals sought to do the same in Britain. Our 'Welfare State 1.0'.

They won the election by a Landslide: 129 seats, a Great Endorsement. When the new parliament opened, the defeated Balfour (who had lost his seat, but had hurriedly been found another one) began an old-fashioned speech, long on rhetorical devices but short on policy. "Enough of this tomfoolery!" CB interrupted in his strong Perthshire accent. There was work to be done.

Acts were passed to encourage local authorities to give children free meals, to remove the rule that made trade unions liable for employers' loss of income during strikes, and to give compensation for workplace injuries. The Programme's budget introduced progressive taxation to prepare for planned bigger, more expensive reforms – the Programme, in its Pomp, could take its time.

Sadly, the health of CB and his wife both began to suffer, and the Programme's first Leader ended up having to hand over to Asquith. Asquith has gone down in history as a great PM, but he was haughty and decidedly illiberal in at least one major policy area, that of female suffrage (CB had been a supporter of that cause, but had felt he would not be able to get the measure passed in parliament). Asquith was lucky to have a truly great Foil, David Lloyd George, who became Chancellor in April 1908.

The Big Wins continued to flow. 1908 saw the introduction of old-age pensions for the over 70s. At the other end of life, a 'Children's Charter' protected the poorest children from various kinds of exploitation. In 1909, labour exchanges were set up, to simplify the process whereby the unemployed could find jobs and where expanding employers could find workers. The 1909 Housing and Town Planning Act stopped the building of any more slums. The 1911 National Insurance Act created both sick pay and unemployment benefit: to qualify, one had to pay 4d a week into a fund, which the government and employers both then topped up.

By later standards, these measures were insufficient – especially when the Great Depression of the 1930s struck. The benefits weren't universal: many people fell through the net, and the sickness and unemployment benefits only lasted 26 and 15 weeks respectively. Not many people made it to 70 then, either. But at the time the reforms were regarded with horror by both Conservatives and old-fashioned Gladstonians as dangerously radical. A Political Programme has to be judged in relation to its era.

In order to pay for them, Lloyd George introduced his People's Budget of 1909. The free-trade Liberals would have nothing to do with import tariffs, and sought to raise revenue by taxing higher incomes and profits on land deals. The Conservatives, massively outvoted in the Commons, decided to fight this in the Lords, where they had a majority. This was unconstitutional – the Upper House was allowed to amend, but not reject, a financial bill. The Lords rejected it. The result was a constitutional standoff, which lasted for over a year until the Lords eventually caved in. This was the Big Battle for the Programme. Asquith and Lloyd George cemented their victory with the 1911 Parliament Act, which took away the Lords' power to veto any bill. Big Battles have to be fought to the end.

The Programme arguably had its Crowning Glory with the enormous success of the 1908 London Olympics, where Britain came top of the medals table by a mile. However, the event was marred by rows between the American team and the hosts – and were the games a celebration of New Liberalism or something more atavistic and nationalist? Lord Desborough, who had been the driving force behind their organization, was a lapsed Gladstonian Liberal who had crossed the floor to the Tories some years back.

More obviously in tune with the Programme's radicalism was the rise of modernism in high culture. This was a rejection of traditions of all kinds and their replacement with emotional intensity, innovation and experiment. It was optimistic – old shackles were going to be thrown off and people would find more freedom to grow (that ultimate New Liberal value) in their creative, intellectual and personal lives. Technology would play its part: early modernists were excited by fast cars and aeroplanes, not just by ideas and art. (After World War One, modernism became darker and more rarefied, but in the New Liberal era, modernists were bright adventurers.)

A classic mixing-ground of New Liberal ideas and the new culture was the magazine *The English Review,* founded in 1908, the year of Asquith's accession to power, by novelist and critic Ford Madox Hueffer (who later changed his surname to Ford). A classic physical meeting place for the two was the residence of Lady Ottoline Morrell in Bloomsbury – her husband was New Liberal MP Philip Morrell.

Looking back on the time, Virginia Woolf, a member of that set, would write, 'On or about December 1910 human character changed.' She was being deliberately provocative with that precision, but her basic point was that, just as New Liberalism had swept away the hierarchy and passivity of the previous Programme, a new sensibility of 'sunshine and fresh air' had entered the nation's life.

However, there was a strong Counterblast. Many more people read the expanding, and strongly Conservative, popular press, the *Daily Mail* and the *Daily Express*, than *The English Review* or even the Liberal *Manchester Guardian*. Rudyard Kipling, who had won the Nobel Prize for Literature in 1907, was, like Salisbury, a vociferous opponent of Home Rule for Ireland, as epitomized in his 1912 rant, *Ulster*.

Roger Fry's *Manet and the Post-Impressionists* exhibition, which unleashed daring, colourful artists like Van Gogh and Matisse on the British public, is a good barometer of the cultural clash of the time. The five Conservative-supporting newspapers attacked it vigorously, berating the works' un-Englishness and comparing their spirit to that of political anarchism. Three of the four Liberal-supporting papers came out in its favour, the *Daily Graphic* commenting that 'the gallery was thronged… Public taste is advancing faster than the critics'.'

In music, Stravinsky's modernist ballet *The Firebird* was first performed in London in 1912. It proved popular with music-lovers. His darker, more dissonant *The Rite of Spring* was more divisive. The *Telegraph* bemoaned the latter's 'primitiveness', commenting, 'such stuff should be played on primeval instruments – or, better, not played at all.'

No description of the culture of the era would be complete without mentioning Bernard Shaw and HG Wells. They were allies of the New Liberals in their opposition to Victorian values, but were proposing a more radical, Socialist solution to the ills of the day. No doubt New Liberal supporters enjoyed their works, except when they started banging the Socialist drum too loudly. Arguably, Wells' Mr Polly, a downtrodden draper with intellectual and aesthetic ambitions, is the New Liberal Archetype.

The New Liberal Programme had a long Pomp. Its huge majority vanished in 1910, when two elections were held, but thanks to the loyal support of Southern Irish MPs it retained its parliamentary power.

In 1912, it managed a Great Escape when almost all its key players were caught up in a scandal involving insider trading in the Marconi Company. Shares had been bought just before the announcement of a government contract. Asquith was not involved, and backed his team members who had been implicated. The furore died down.

Slow Stranglers were beginning to emerge, however. Suffragism grew ever more militant, and the official reaction to it became ever more oppressive. Asquith refused to countenance electoral reform – an example of a Programme being threatened by a blind spot in its vision (or, in this case, the vision of its Leader).

Ireland became ever more polarized, with Gladstonian moves towards Home Rule being matched by rising militancy in Ulster. In March 1914, British forces threatened to mutiny if told to fire on Ulster militia.

Industrial relations deteriorated. The period from 1910 to 1914 is referred to as the 'Great Unrest'. Despite the good intentions of the government, some monopoly employers had kept wages low for much of the new century. A wave of strikes hit the country. Ones in the Rhondda Valley in 1910/11 and Liverpool in 1911 became particularly violent, and the army was sent in to restore order. Churchill, Home Secretary at the time, has still not been forgiven in parts of South Wales.

However, none of these ended up destroying the Programme. Historian Lord Kenneth Morgan writes that the Liberal government 'was still powerful in 1914'. It was working on reforms, and still had what Morgan calls 'the zest to govern'.

What destroyed it were war and the change of mood that came as the nation became aware of what that really entailed.

Neither Asquith nor Lloyd George wanted war. After the assassination of the Archduke Franz Ferdinand on 28th June 1914, Asquith had written that there was 'no reason why we should be anything more than spectators' in any resulting European conflict. His Chancellor had added that 'there are always clouds in the international sky'. But once the PM had rejected the idea of officially promising not to take part in such a conflict, events spiralled out of control, and hostilities broke out, 37 days after the shooting.

That was the Programme's last Great Escape. War was not greeted with dismay or resignation but by a rush of patriotic fervour. This was just another continental spat. Given Britain's military and naval might, it would all be over by Christmas.

The first Big Failure (hardly the fault of the Programme, but the first major divergence between its Worldview and reality) came when the numerically superior Russians, expected to sweep into Germany from the East, were trounced at the Battle of Tannenberg, an event graphically described in Alexander Solzhenitsyn's *August 1914*.

On the western front, things took a different turn. There was no big breakthrough by either side, and the armies began building trenches. By Christmas, these extended over 450 miles from the Channel to the Swiss

Alps. This was the Body-blow to the Programme, born in a time of peace but now an irrelevance in the new world that had suddenly emerged, one of mass slaughter by machine-gun and of total war by attrition.

In May 1915, a British offensive at Aubers Ridge, near Béthune, achieved nothing and over 11,000 men were killed or wounded (the Germans lost less than 1,000). A shortage of shells was blamed for the disaster. Asquith concluded that the Liberals could not govern alone and asked the Conservatives to form a Coalition. The Conservatives agreed – ironically, one of their conditions for this was that Churchill should be removed from the War Cabinet. The new government took over on 25th May. This marked the Dethronement of the New Liberal Programme. It no longer controlled events or chimed with the national mood, though, as it was nominally still in power, could still be blamed when things went wrong.

Taxes, of course, had to rise to pay for the conflict. Lloyd George raised income tax substantially, and also introduced a tax on 'Excess Profits' that businesses made above an agreed pre-war level. But much funding came from ballooning debt.

In 1916, the progress of the war went from bad to worse, with the collapse of the Gallipoli campaign in January, the disastrous defeat at Kut-al-Amara in Mesopotamia in April, and the carnage at the Somme on July 1st. Asquith's personal star faded, too. In September 1916 his eldest son, Raymond, was killed at the Battle of Flers–Courcelette. His difficulties with alcohol escalated (our word 'squiffy' comes from him). On the political front, he faced more and more dilemmas, as the war required ever more illiberal moves such as the introduction of conscription. The popular press had it in for him.

In December of that dreadful year, the once-mighty all-reforming New

Liberal Programme met its Waterloo, being put out of its misery by the man who had once been its driving force, Lloyd George (I shall describe how in the next chapter). The Dissolution of the Programme followed. In the 1918 election, Asquith's section of a by then long-split party would win a measly 36 seats. This number would not include Asquith.

The decline of New Liberalism was charted by historian George Dangerfield in a book with the haunting title *The Strange Death of Liberal England*. However, the death of Liberal England was no stranger than that of any of the Political Programmes described in this book. They are all mortal, bound by the same rule that the Worldview that once made them great and original becomes a disastrous set of blinkers as events move on.

New Liberalism

Provisional Leader: Henry Campbell-Bannerman ('CB')

Leader: Herbert Asquith

Foil: David Lloyd George

The Villain: Inescapable poverty

The Bright Future: Freedom from poverty will allow people to fulfil themselves

Core Policies: 'Welfare State 1.0', Free Trade, Home Rule for Ireland

Crucible Group: Rainbow Circle

Sacred Texts: *Lecture on Liberal Legislation and Freedom of Contract* (TH Green), Booth and Rowntree reports, *Liberalism* (Hobhouse)

Gaining Significant Influence: CB becomes party leader 1899 / his 'methods of barbarism' speech, 1901

First Taste of Power: Minority government of 1905

Great Endorsement: 129 seat victory in 1906

Cultural Endorsement: Modernism, *The English Review, Manet and the Post-Impressionists* exhibition, *The History of Mr Polly*

Cultural Counterblasts: The popular press, *Ulster* (Kipling)

Big Wins: Introduction of many welfare measures, People's Budget

Big Battle: With House of Lords

Great Escapes: Marconi Scandal, outbreak of war

Slow Stranglers (in peacetime): Ireland, suffragette movement, industrial unrest

First Big Failure: German victory on Eastern front, August 1914

Body-blow: The emerging nature of the war, September to December 1914

Dethronement: Entering Coalition, May 1915

Waterloo: Lloyd George becomes PM, December 1916

Lloyd George 1
The Knock-out Blow: 1916 to 1918

It took over two years from the assassination of the Archduke for a true war-winning Political Programme to take power. Even in the face of crying need, political change can be slow.

'Take power' is what it did. The electorate could not speak in the middle of the conflict, so change came, as it had to, via a Palace Revolution, which took place in two stages. The first dethroned the struggling old Programme, but still in a way that the new Programme's grasp on power was provisional. The second fully and irrevocably installed the new one.

The first part of the Palace Revolution, detailed in the last section, was the administration's entry into coalition in May 1915. After that, Asquith was still PM but what we would now call a 'lame duck'. Never a war leader – he was assiduous but lacked the bravado necessary at such a time – he was no longer the centre of energy, which is what a Programme Leader must be. That was now his former Foil, Lloyd George, whose temperament fitted the new era perfectly. In the new administration, the Welshman moved from being Chancellor to Minister of Munitions. This might seem like a demotion, but given the fury at the shell shortage at Aubers Ridge, that was then the most important role in the government. He rose to the challenge. Munitions had previously been the responsibility of the military; he seized control from them. He got industrialists involved. He encouraged the employment of women in munitions factories (he promised them the vote in return, a Core pledge that he duly honoured). There were no more shell shortages.

Elsewhere, however, the mishaps mentioned in the previous section – Gallipoli, Kut, the Somme – befell the Programme. Late 1916 saw various political manoeuvrings, led by Lloyd George (who had been made Secretary of State for War in June), Tory leader Andrew Bonar Law and newspaper proprietor Max Aitken. The Conservatives refused to serve under Asquith. He resigned on 5th December, and a new Coalition was formed, with some Liberals, the Conservatives and Labour (who were persuaded to join by a speech from Lloyd George). On the 7th, the 'cottage-born' Welshman became PM.

This second stage of the Great War Palace Revolution was the equivalent of an electoral Great Endorsement. From then on, Lloyd George had all the power he needed, to do whatever he (and his new Programme) wanted – within the UK, of course. On the fields of Flanders or the high seas, he had less control, though he battled with the top brass over strategy (Asquith's approach had been to let the military men run things as they thought fit).

The new Programme was utterly different from its predecessor. Its Big Idea was brutally simple: to fight the war to the end and win it with 'a knock-out blow', whatever the cost. If Lloyd George, the former New Liberal Chancellor, was its Leader, its tone and its parliamentary muscle came from the Conservatives. The War Cabinet that he formed featured three Conservatives, a Socialist and himself: not an Asquithian Liberal in sight. That didn't mean that Lloyd George instantly lost his spiky Celtic radicalism, but it did mean that his radicalism was focused in a new direction. The war became a moral crusade, a fight against the absolute evil instantiated by the Kaiser's Germany. Only total defeat could expunge such evil – and result in the end of war forever, as the forces of virtue would have won.

This events-driven Programme had not had time to emerge from a Crucible Group. Lloyd George did the next best thing, and formed a virtual one on acceding to power, a group of close advisors that became known as his 'Garden Suburb'. This was a small collection of diverse talents (which is what Crucible Groups should be): a diplomat, an academic, two Welsh MPs, a plutocrat and the Welsh wizard himself.

A few days after this martial, vigorous new Programme seized power, the Germans made a peace offer to the allies via US President Woodrow Wilson. It was couched in haughty terms and was probably unacceptable – but it is an interesting debate as to what might have happened if it had been made, not to the Leader of a Programme right at the start of its Pomp, but instead to an older, degenerating administration created for peace, not total war. Such an administration could have used the offer as a starting-point for negotiations. Had these been successful and a peace been achieved, there would have been no Passchendaele. There might have been no Russian Revolution. There would probably have been no Spanish flu, which was spread by troop movements and preyed on a people weakened by war. There would certainly have been no Treaty of Versailles. Adolf Hitler would have most likely ended up an irate nobody, ranting at anybody who would listen – till they got bored – in downmarket Munich beer cellars. But that is speculation. The offer was refused, and the war ground on. And on and on and on.

Culturally, the new Programme was buoyed up by expressions of martial patriotism. The most notable include James Clark's painting *The Great Sacrifice*, showing a soldier at the foot of Christ on the Cross, *In Flanders Fields*, a poem in rondeau form by Canadian medic John McCrae, and the famous recruiting posters – Lord Kitchener pointing at the viewer, Saville Lumley's *Daddy, what did YOU do in the Great War?* Interestingly, these works predate the actual seizure of power by the Programme. The

Zeitgeist, born in the trenches, was, as often, ahead of politics. The Programme's Archetype was already out there, among the mud, barbed wire and shell holes.

Once dominant, much of the Programme's official culture would be even more heavy-handed and somehow less memorable, ramming home its message that Germany represented absolute evil and we were fighting for absolute good.

Much more lasting was the Counterblast produced by the great anti-war poets of the era: civilized, sensitive young men horrified by the mechanized brutality of the Western front.

There were also the marching songs. These often have an ambivalence to them. *It's a Long Way to Tipperary* is not about the evil of the German state or the wonders of British military power, but about home and the desire to return there. *Mademoiselle from Armentières* is even less imbued with patriotism. The more jingoistic *Belgium put the Kybosh on the Kaiser* was popular till Christmas 1914, after which its popularity waned.

The Programme can claim a number of Big Wins. At home, the economy was put on a war footing, ending the delusion suffered by the old Programme that this was an old-fashioned conflict that could be fought with little domestic disruption (there had been some piecemeal intervention in the economy by the previous Programme, but the new one took this to a new level. For example, by the end of the war the government bought and distributed 80% of the nation's food.) In 1918, the Programme finally laid the ghost of Asquith and introduced female suffrage.

Most historians say that Lloyd George's interventions in military strategy were successful. Some say he should have intervened even more, for example sacking Haig before the Passchendaele campaign, which Lloyd George later described as 'senseless'. His insistence on using the convoy system for Atlantic merchant shipping, against the desires of the Admiralty, neutered the U-boats that, in early 1917, had threatened to starve the country. When the German Army threatened to break through the Western front in early 1918, he forced the military to accept a unified overall command.

Big Wins, that saved many lives. But, of course, the real Big Win, and the only one that truly mattered, came at 11.00 on 11th November 1918. The knock-out blow was delivered.

Lloyd George 1
The Knock-out Blow

Leader: David Lloyd George

Villain: Germany

The Bright Future: Winning 'the war to end all wars'

Archetype: The soldier on the Western front

Core Policies: No negotiation with Germany. Centralized state power, including of LG over military

First Taste of Power: Coalition, May 1915

Great Endorsement: Palace Revolution of December 1916

Crucible Group (post-victory): The 'Garden Suburb'

Cultural Endorsement: *The Great Sacrifice, In Flanders Fields*

Cultural Counterblasts: The great War Poets, the more subversive marching songs

Big Battle: With Germany

Big Wins: Creating a genuine war economy, Atlantic convoy system, unified command, votes for women – and, finally, Victory

Lloyd George 2
'A Fit Country for Heroes to Live in', 1918 - 22

Normally a Political Programme never quits in the middle of its Pomp. Why would it? But with the war won, this one had achieved its aim. Just as there had been in August 1914, there was a whole new world to deal with.

The Leader of the old Programme used the huge national support he had to create a second one. This had its own Big Idea, 'to make Britain a Fit Country for Heroes to Live in'. The Villain was still Imperial Germany, but a new threat was included in the First Stories, that of Bolshevism.

An election was held as soon as possible after the armistice. The tone changed during the campaign, with initial, optimistic Liberalism giving way to an angrier determination to 'squeeze the German lemon until the pips squeak' (a stump quote from a Conservative, Eric Geddes, which Lloyd George adopted). This reversion to Conservative Triumphalism was a bad omen for the Welshman's Programme. Who was really going to call the shots? Political Programmes may tweak their messages during election campaigns, but they don't introduce, then prioritize, radically new ones.

The reversion worked in the short term. On election day (14th December) Lloyd George's coalition received a massive Endorsement – one that made the 1906 Landslide look like a gentle nod of approval. However, Conservatives were the majority in the coalition. Led by Bonar

Law but accepting 'the man who won the war' as PM, they had 332 seats. Liberals who supported Lloyd George (the 'Coalition Liberals') had 127. For the opposition, Labour had 57 seats and the old Asquithian Liberals 36. Almost all of Southern Ireland voted for the new, more radically separatist party of Sinn Fein, who refused to sit in the Commons. The coalition had huge power – but to do what, exactly?

It set out, as the PM intended, with a Liberal agenda. The school leaving age was raised to 14. An act subsidised local authorities to build houses – housebuilding had not been seen as a government responsibility before. National Insurance was extended to more workers. Former New Liberal Christopher Addison was made Minister of Health, a new position charged with improving public wellbeing. Old-age pensions were increased and offered to blind people over 50. Working hours were reduced.

The issue of Ireland, an old Liberal cause, was finally settled. The road to that settlement was bloody in the extreme, with what was effectively a war between the IRA and British forces breaking out in 1919. But Lloyd George managed to negotiate an agreement between the furious antagonists – something that none of his predecessors had been able to do. Despite the bloodshed before the agreement and the fact that it still had to be finalized (bitter disputes remained about the precise boundaries of the two Irelands), some historians regard this as his finest achievement. It was certainly a Big Win.

The PM's negotiating skills were less in evidence in the lead-up to the Treaty of Versailles. Despite his Triumphalism during the election, he had a nuanced understanding of the situation, writing in private: 'If she [Germany] feels she has been unjustly treated… she will find means of exacting retribution from her conquerors'. However, he encountered a

French delegation as greedy for vengeance as his own public self and an American one with unrealistically high ideals which was soon ignored. He ended up signing a treaty that he must have known would be disastrous. Despite this, he was welcomed as a hero returning from the negotiations. This was a Great Escape, a grievous policy mistake not picked up on at the time.

The Culture of the era was, naturally, steeped in trauma. The Programme sought to soothe this: the aim was to get life back to some kind of normality. The most famous expression of this was Edward Lutyens' simple, dignified Cenotaph in the middle of Whitehall. The one we see today is not the original. That was made of wood and plaster; it was meant to be temporary, one small aspect of the massive Victory parade to be held in July 1919 (though the War ended on 11/11, celebrations were muted until the signing of the Versailles Treaty on 28th June 1919). However, it immediately became a place of pilgrimage, with over a million people coming to lay flowers in the week after the parade. It was retained. Wreaths were laid at it on November 11th of that year. A permanent version, made from Portland Stone, was then commissioned. The formal unveiling, on November 11th, 1920, was another mass event, with people queuing for hours to pay respects to the 'Glorious Dead'.

These huge outpourings of public grief were a kind of melancholic Crowning Glory for the Programme, an expression of shared emotion and national pride that chimed with the Programme's initial cross-party nature and the determination of the man who won the war to do the right thing by the survivors of that conflict.

The solidity of the Cenotaph was in strong contrast to other works of this brief era, which can be seen as Counterblasts. Modernism took a darker, madder turn. 'It is not proper or sensible to paint after such an experience,' said Stanley Spencer on returning from the front, though he would later change his mind. Artists saw reality as fractured and arbitrary. The bitterest art of the era probably came from the war's losers – Käthe Kollwitz or Georg Grosz – but paintings like William Orpen's *Blown Up,* John Singer Sergeant's *Gassed* or Paul Nash's *Menin Road* have their own sense of horror. Nash said of his painting that he wanted to 'rob the war of its last shred of glory'.

In music, a new genre smashed old certainties to smithereens, not so much opposing the existing culture but proposing a radical alternative. The Original Dixieland Jazz Band began a tour of the UK in April 1919. It set heads spinning and feet tapping, but the band's leader and cornettist, Nick LaRocca, was a troubled, angry individual, befitting this pained era.

The economy behaved more like a modernist smash-up than the dignified Cenotaph. There was a brief febrile boom in 1919, accompanied by soaring inflation. This quickly turned to a bust, with the number of unemployed rocketing. Time for the Programme to fully show its Liberal colours and support these people…

The popular press and the Conservatives began insisting the expensive reforms be turned back and the nation's books be balanced. There was, after all, a huge debt now overhanging the nation… Given the parliamentary arithmetic, Lloyd George had no option but to agree. Addison was sacked in April 1921, and in August of that year, Eric Geddes, of 'squeeze the pips' fame, was brought in to make cuts. These were swingeing, and became known as the Geddes Axe. The Axe cut the Liberal heart out of the Programme. It was the Programme's Body-blow, its fatal U-turn.

The Programme was now limping along. Accusations of corruption surfaced: honours had been sold to fund a future new party (a peerage would set you back over £50,000). Lloyd George was offered a massive advance for his memoirs, which many people considered an insult to war victims. The final straw was a crisis in Turkey, in September 1922. Turkish troops were advancing on Chanak, a British outpost in the north-west of the country. Lloyd George wanted to go to war to defend it (as did Churchill). Some Liberals and most Conservatives did not, and in the end, a peaceful settlement was negotiated. Lloyd George had lost the last of his authority over the administration. The Coalition collapsed.

An election was held that November, which the Conservatives won by a healthy-looking majority. That majority was not to last, but the Liberal Party would not be the winner next time round – or ever again (at time of writing, anyway). Ironically, the Liberals had the two most influential political thinkers of the era that followed, John Maynard Keynes and William Beveridge, in its ranks – which shows, sadly, that having great individual thinkers is not a sufficient condition of political success.

After the loss, Lloyd George tried to reunite the Liberals, but Asquith (back in parliament) and his supporters had had enough of him. As a back-bencher, he returned to his more radical self. The Liberal Party continued its Dissolution.

The relatively short life of this Programme also shows that it takes more than a Leader, however charismatic, to create a lasting Political Programme. There is talk of modern British politics becoming more 'presidential'. This chapter is a reminder that this is not new – and that our previous experiment with such politics did not last long.

Lloyd George 2
'A Fit Country for Heroes to Live in'

Leader: David Lloyd George

Core Policy: Continuing expansion of Welfare State

Archetype: Demobbed warrior

Villains: Imperial Germany, Bolshevism

The Great Endorsement: Massive Coalition victory in 1918 election

Cultural Endorsement: Edwin Lutyens, *The Cenotaph*

Crowning Glory: Public pilgrimages to Cenotaph in 1919 and 1920

Counterblasts: *Blown Up*, William Orpen. *Menin Road*, Paul Nash

Big Wins: Early 'New Liberal' measures, initial post-war boom,
    a settlement in Ireland

Great Escape: Conceding too much to the French at Versailles

Slow Strangler: Lack of parliamentary majority for LG's ideas

Body-blow: Geddes Axe

Dethronement: Conservatives quit the Coalition, October 1922

Waterloo: Conservative Landslide, 1924. Liberal split becomes
    permanent

Tranquillity, 1922 - 1940

The Conservative Party had been out for blood between 1914 and 1918. Always the master of self-reinvention, in 1922 it recreated itself around the Big Idea of peace. 'We should have tranquillity and stability both at home and abroad,' said Bonar Law in his election address. The Conservative manifesto for the 1922 election became known as the Tranquillity Manifesto.

At the same time, some material was carried forward from the previous Programme. Bolshevism remained a serious Villain, and respect for the War dead remained a core emotion. Older Tory themes were also carried forward. Bonar Law's observation that 'The nation's first need... is, in every walk of life, to get on with its work with the minimum of interference at home and of disturbance abroad' could have been made by Lord Salisbury.

There does not seem to have been a Crucible Group for this Programme. The nearest approach, perhaps, is a meeting at the Carlton Club held in October 1922, when the party's MPs met to decide whether to ditch the Coalition with the Lloyd George Liberals after the Chanak crisis. After a particularly impressive speech by Stanley Baldwin, they voted to do so. The policy manifesto was written in some haste after that – but proved very durable.

Similarly, there is no powerful Canon for the Programme – though when I think of it, I am reminded of Conservative philosopher Edmund Burke's lines, written back in 1790: "Because half a dozen grasshoppers under a fern make the field ring with their importunate chink, whilst thousands of great cattle, reposed beneath the shadow of the British oak, chew the cud and are silent, pray do not imagine that those who make the noise are the only inhabitants of the field."

Baldwin, the man who would end up as the Programme Leader, was a not a theorist but a practical businessman with a streak of rural romanticism and a strong Christian faith. Of all the Leaders in this story, he is the least personally ambitious. He went into politics out of a sense of duty. When politicians start talking about their eagerness to serve the public, eyebrows are usually raised, but in Baldwin's case this does seem to have been his central motivation. He was lucky, too, of course. He didn't have to scramble up the first part of the greasy pole. His father, Alfred, had been an MP and had died young; Stanley was expected to step into his shoes and duly did so. He then found he was rather good at politics, like a child gifted an old guitar who turns out to have a real talent for songwriting.

The Carlton Club meeting can be seen as the moment of the Programme's gaining Significant Influence. The election win, the First Taste of Power for the new Programme, followed almost immediately afterwards, in November.

The majority of the win – 74 seats – might look like an instant Great Endorsement. But it wasn't. Things don't usually work that fast. The Conservative Party was still recovering from its relationship with the tempestuous Lloyd George. The man who had led the party to its new victory, Bonar Law, was in poor health, and Baldwin, who soon replaced him, had to learn the game quickly. He did, but not quickly enough. Rather than tough out a potentially party-splitting plan to ditch free trade and embrace tariffs and 'Imperial Preference', he decided to go to the polls – and lost his majority. David Cameron's attempt to mend his party's split over Europe by holding a referendum leaps to mind as a modern parallel.

A new Aspirant Programme then got its First Taste of Power, but failed to translate that into a Great Endorsement. This wasn't just the First Taste of Power for a new Programme but for a new party: Labour. However, it was not a success. Given the parliamentary arithmetic – it did not win a majority – it had very little chance of so being. All the Programme's leader, Ramsay Macdonald, could do was show that his new party could govern responsibly and aim for a proper Endorsement at a future election. It made some progress, domestically via the Wheatley Act that mandated the building of more social housing, and abroad via attempts to calm the continuing French determination to crucify Germany. But it was always going to need a proper mandate, and after ten months, it asked the electorate for one. Its request was not granted. In the election held in October 1924, Baldwin returned, now with his own Landslide Great Endorsement, a massive 210 seat majority.

It was as if he had never left. The Tranquillity Programme was calmly reinstated and government went on as in 1922/3, though now in its Pomp.

The Programme enjoyed its Crowning Glory at the British Empire Exhibition of 1924/5 (part of the Expo ran during the Macdonald administration, but it had been a child of the Tranquillity Programme and was a perfect expression of it). Visitors – adults paid 1/6, children 9d – could stroll round the huge site in Wembley and visit opulent Pavilions from 56 territories in the Empire (the one from Canada featured a statue of the Prince of Wales carved from butter) or 'Palaces' of Industry, Engineering and Arts. They could enjoy the boating lake, funfair, numerous restaurants and a nightly Pageant of Empire featuring 15,000 performers. The tone of the exhibition was imperialist, but, in tune with 'Tranquillity', celebrated an Empire that worked amicably together. A family of nations. There were no Maxim guns on display.

The Programme had a strong Cultural Endorsement. The Archetype was the gentleman, a role epitomized by Baldwin himself. A true gentleman – like a Baldwin voter – could come from any class. He was polite, listened to others' views, didn't score cheap points off anyone and took others' interests into consideration when acting. If he had an advantage, social or physical, he never used it unfairly or maliciously. The lady by his side was similar.

However, in practice the notion was often tied up with upper middle-class snobbery. The gents in the popular literature of the time all came from this stratum. In Warwick Deeping's 1925 bestseller *Sorrell and Son,* an impoverished army officer, returned from the trenches, makes huge sacrifices to ensure his son has the private education that will make him a gentleman. Gents in popular thrillers, from the rather decent Richard Hannay to the racist thug Bulldog Drummond, were all quite posh (full-on aristos were a bit suspect), though often, like Captain Stephen Sorrell MC, short of cash.

Ladies do not come well out of *Sorrell and Son* or the adventures of Bulldog Drummond, but find a more sympathetic niche in the era's 'Golden Age' detective stories, where their superior understanding of human nature enables them to solve crimes that baffle blundering, fact-bound male police officers.

At a more highbrow level, the Programme's sensibilities were mirrored by Georgian poets such as John Drinkwater and John Masefield. The

Georgian movement had begun before the Great War, but reached the apex of its popularity during the Baldwin years. The poems are formally correct: they rhyme and scan. They are romantic, outdoors-y, slightly wistful and very English. The compositions of Ralph Vaughan Williams have a similar sense. *The Lark Ascending* is Baldwinism set to music.

Counterblasts? 'Hot', improvisatory jazz, in the Original Dixieland style, continued to cock a hedonistic snook at Baldwinian worthiness (the more scripted, 'sweet' jazz, played by big bands like Jack Hylton or the Savoy Orpheans, was more in tune with the Programme). Many writers and artists made clear Counterblast turns to the left, especially as the 1920s turned into the 1930s. Novelist/critic DJ Taylor refers to the 1930s as 'the Pink Decade'. George Orwell's *The Road to Wigan Pier*, published in 1937, showed that despite Baldwin's genuine desire to heal the class divide, his Programme hadn't done nearly enough. The PM's vision, formed in his family's paternalistic (and extremely successful) medium-size provincial ironworks, didn't map onto the nation as a whole, where entire sectors were in decline and old class antagonisms ran deep.

A few other writers, like poet Ezra Pound, had equal contempt for Baldwinian gentlemanliness but veered off to the far right.

In 1925, the Programme scored its first Big Win by sorting out the borders of Northern Ireland. This was a fraught issue, with a very real threat of a return to violence if negotiations failed. Baldwin, like Lloyd George, was a skilled negotiator, and masterminded a settlement acceptable to both sides. He wrote 'pax pacem' in the Chequers visitors' book (where the negotiations had been held) after the participants had left. All he was saying was give peace a chance.

On the international front, the same year saw Britain sign the Treaty of Locarno, establishing Germany's Western borders and effectively readmitting Germany, now under the liberal Weimar republic, to the family of nations. Tranquillity could now reign in Europe, too.

An early Great Escape was the return to the gold standard, a measure that kept the pound fixed at a rate that was far too high, which made British goods hard to sell abroad. However, the electorate did not punish this, and the move would be reversed in 1931.

The Programme's Big Battle? This was the General Strike of May 1926, fought against left-wing, unionized labour.

Baldwin did the fighting in his own way. In his 1924 election victory speech, he spoke of his ambition "to make one nation of our own people which, if secured, nothing else matters in the world". (The slogan 'one nation' is often attributed to Victorian Conservative PM Benjamin Disraeli, but 'Dizzy' never used it: it was Baldwin who first did so.) Baldwin divided his opponents, making a distinction between the dispute with the miners which had started it off, which he settled with negotiations, and the wider strike, which he saw as an expression of unacceptable extremism, 'an attempt to take over the function of the Government by a body that has not been elected'.

On the day the strike collapsed, Baldwin broadcast to the nation: "Our business is not to triumph over those who have failed in a mistaken attempt." Baldwin didn't do Triumphalism. Instead, he chatted calmly and reasonably to listeners to the ever more popular radio, as if he were sitting in an armchair next to them, puffing away at his pipe.

In May 1929, it was time for another election. Baldwin campaigned with a suitably tranquil slogan, 'Safety First'. Essentially, what happened was a re-run of 1922/4. The electorate decided Baldwin was a bit dull, voted for someone else, but soon changed its mind.

The result of the 1929 election was a First Taste of Power for a second Aspirant Labour Programme. It had no outright majority, but (unlike in 1922) was the biggest party in the House. A minority government was duly sworn in, and set about a programme of public works.

It was appallingly unlucky. The election had been held in May; on October 24th, the previously booming US stock market suffered a major sell-off. The Wall Street Crash had begun. The Great Depression would follow. The economy went into a slump. Unemployment began to soar. A Committee set up under Sir George May, former Secretary of Prudential Insurance, recommended massive cuts to government expenditure, including unemployment benefit. Keynes said it was 'The most foolish document I ever had the misfortune to read' – but nobody was listening to him. Just as Lloyd George had done in 1921/2, the new Aspirant Labour Programme did a violent U-turn and voted to follow May's advice – a self-inflicted Body-blow. The party split, a luxury that no minority administration can afford.

Macdonald, still Labour leader, tried to form a National Government with the Conservatives. He was pressurized into testing this new administration at the polls, now standing against his old party (something that has never been forgiven by the left). In the 1931 election, the National Government won a massive majority of 497. A victory for Macdonald? Almost all the 'National' candidates were Conservatives, and they called the tune. They did so in a suitably tranquil way, of course. Baldwin liked Macdonald and was happy to work with him. But when illness forced Macdonald to retire in 1935, who else was there to step into his shoes, but the man who had effectively been in charge all along? Back to business as usual.

That business seemed largely successful. There was growing prosperity in south and central England. Light engineering flourished and more people moved into higher-paid, salaried work. The Programme's real Big Win was the suburbia that sprawled out from Britain's major cities, where millions of a newly well-off middle class genuinely found leafy-laned tranquillity.

But Slow Stranglers were at work.

If parts of Britain were flourishing, others weren't. The era of Baldwin's Programme has become associated with poverty, exemplified by the Jarrow march of October 1936, which was the culmination of years of underemployment in a declining industry, shipbuilding. The Programme seemed to have no remedy for this.

An even more vicious Strangler was the Programme's inability to deal with the rising threat of fascism. It is a core theme of this book that, as events never stand still, Political Programmes, which can't change their core beliefs and policies without becoming meaningless, are doomed to become outdated. This happened to Tranquillity with particular harshness.

In the mid-1930s, the two European fascist states both started pushing at the established international order.

During 1935, Mussolini steadily increased military pressure on Ethiopia (then called Abyssinia). The League of Nations did virtually nothing to stop him. In October of that year, he invaded. Britain and France tried to undermine what efforts the League had been making to punish Italy, by trying to do a secret deal with the invaders. (Baldwin was not party to this attempted deal, which was cobbled together by his Foreign Secretary Samuel Hoare and the future head of the Vichy regime Pierre Laval, on a trip by Hoare to Paris that Baldwin thought was a holiday.) When the truth came out, there was fury, though it was more the underhand nature of the deal than the deal itself that was disliked. Former Chancellor Austen Chamberlain provided the ultimate 'Tranquillity' put-down: "Gentlemen don't behave in such a way." The Hoare-Laval Pact was scrapped.

After a lull over the Christmas period, the Italians stepped up hostilities. A key battle was the capture of the strategically important mountain of Ambra Aradam on 19th February 1936. Mustard gas was sprayed on the fleeing Ethiopians.

Hitler, who had been quietly observing the proceedings, noted the world's lack of response, and marched into the Rhineland on March 5th. This was in direct contravention of the Treaty of Versailles. Again, nothing was done.

In retrospect, letting the dictators do this was disastrous. But there was little popular or elite support for military action at that time, in the UK or in the country with whom this standing up would have jointly to be done, France. These have to qualify as Great Escapes: policy mistakes that went unpunished at the time.

It wasn't till mid-1937 that Labour's National Executive finally agreed to stop voting against defence expenditure. The claim, later made, that the bulldog British people were eager for war in the late 1930s but doddering old Baldwin refused to listen, is grossly unfair. The vast majority desperately wanted peace and Baldwin simply stuck to the values of his Programme (created, remember, as a response to the excessive militarism of an earlier era), which is what all Political Programme Leaders do.

Fascism, Naziism and Soviet Communism represented totally new Worldviews and Action Plans that decent democrats like Baldwin (and most of his contemporaries) were completely unable to comprehend. Arguably, they could have done: the Nazi Sacred Text, *Mein Kampf*, had been available in an abridged translation since 1933. But such is the tunnel vision of Political Programmes: a blessing at their start, a curse at their end. And before we judge too harshly – are we being just as complacent about the Climate Emergency right now?

Baldwin retired due to ill health in May 1937, leaving in what diarist Harold Nicholson called a 'blaze of affection'. A Replacement Leader, Neville Chamberlain, half-brother of Austen, took over. Chamberlain was a lesser man than Baldwin: spiky and distant, an effective minister but a poor PM.

Mussolini completed his occupation of Ethiopia: now it was Hitler's turn to keep upping the ante. March 1938 saw the annexation of Austria and his preparations to invade Czechoslovakia. The latter were briefly held up by the Munich agreement of September 1938, signed by Germany, Britain, France and Italy, which ceded the German-speaking parts of that country to Hitler. The agreement was generally praised in Britain at the time. A by-election in Oxford that October was won by a pro-Munich candidate.

The nature of Hitler's domestic policies could no longer be hidden after *Kristallnacht* in November of that year, when SA and Hitler Youth members went on a national rampage, vandalizing Jewish properties and killing Jewish citizens, while the SS rounded up tens of thousands more Jews and put them in camps. In March 1939, the nature of the Führer's foreign policy became equally obvious as he ripped up Chamberlain's piece of paper and invaded the rest of Czechoslovakia. All his previous military ventures had been aimed at drawing ethnically German areas into the national fold. This took his aggressiveness to a new level.

The psychotic violence of *Kristallnacht* and the invasion of the non-German-speaking parts of Czechoslovakia were joint Body-blows to the Programme. The world was no longer tranquil, and now everyone could see this. The mood of the nation changed from one desiring peace to one gearing up for war.

The now-broken Programme limped along for a year after this. Chamberlain was forced to declare war in September 1939 after Germany's next act of international aggression, against Poland. He was ousted in a Palace Revolution in May 1940: the Programme's Dethronement (more about this in the next chapter).

The Tranquillity Programme met its Waterloo almost at once, as it became the butt of vicious and sustained criticism. The book *Guilty Men* appeared in July 1940, which shredded the reputations of 24 'appeasers'. Baldwin was one of them. The Programme's Dissolution began. Its reputation has yet to recover.

Tranquillity

Leader: Stanley Baldwin

Replacement Leader: Neville Chamberlain

Villain: Class politics, especially Bolshevism

The Bright Future: Economic growth in a peaceful world.

Core Policies: Peace treaties in Europe, moderate the class struggle

Gaining Significant Influence: Quitting coalition, October 1922

The First Taste of Power: Election victory, November 1922

The Great Endorsement: 1924 election, 210 majority

Crowning Glory: British Empire Exhibition 1924/5

Great Escapes: Going onto gold standard, 1925; insufficient reply
    to aggression by Mussolini and Hitler, 1935/6

Archetype: English Gentleman (and Lady)

Cultural Endorsement: *Sorrell and Son*, Warwick Deeping, 1925

Counterblast: *The Road to Wigan Pier,* George Orwell, 1937

Big Wins: Irish border settled, Locarno Treaty, suburbia

Big Battle: General strike, 1926

Slow Stranglers: Failure to address poverty, failure to understand
    Fascism/Naziism

Body-blows: *Kristallnacht,* 1938; Hitler invades Czechoslovakia, 1939

Dethronement: Churchill/Attlee Coalition, May 1940

Waterloo: Publication of *Guilty Men,* July 1940

1945 Socialism, 1940 - 1951

I've called the Programme this because 1945 was its *annus mirabilis*, the year of its Great Endorsement. But the Programme was a major force in the land from May 1940 onwards. The idea that the 1945 election Landslide emerged out of nowhere is a myth. Britain was in many ways already a socialist state by then, and had been for five years.

I nearly called the Programme 'Patriotic Communalism', a term used by historian Lord Peter Hennessy. It was certainly both these things. The first is often forgotten. Clement Attlee and his administration carried forward the fierce patriotism of wartime in a way that would make the modern woke left, or even woke's right-on 1980s precursors, squirm. When Ernest Bevin said of the atom bomb "We've got to have a bloody Union Jack on top of it", he wasn't being ironic or postmodern. He meant it. Attlee valued many traditional British institutions. A firm monarchist, he got on well with King George VI. He never disowned his public-school background, retaining a soft spot for his *alma mater*, Haileybury College.

If there was a Crucible Group for the Programme, it met a long time before the Programme took office. After the electoral disaster of 1931 nearly wiped out the Labour Party, Attlee worked with George Lansbury, Stafford Cripps and a group of academics at the LSE led by Harold Laski to formulate an Action Plan. However, time – and practicality – watered down its realization; its Action Plan was much more radical than the policies that were actually put into practice in 1940 or 1945.

There was no real Action Group. Attlee got involved in the Labour Party from his youth and rose though its ranks by hard work and because people liked and trusted him. He acquired Significant Influence when he became its leader in 1935, largely because his rivals for the post had all made enemies in various parts of the party.

He then led the party for two decades. Contrary to the slurs of his detractors, Attlee was a true Leader, not just a placeholder who somehow got stuck in place. His leadership style was different to the modern one, which is why he is often underrated. He stuck quietly, but firmly and consistently, to his views, but allowed himself to be outvoted in cabinet, not because he was weak but because he believed that was the right way to do things. His combination of solidity, utter integrity and personal modesty turned out to be a huge asset. People liked him. Unlike many successful politicians, he had very little vanity or ego.

Arguably there was a huge Canon for this Programme. Victor Gollancz' Left Book Club offered readers one title a month from 1936. But a Canon should be narrowed down to a few specific Sacred Texts.

Attlee's greatest influence was *Looking Backward* by the American writer Edward Bellamy, a story about a Rip van Winkle character who goes to sleep in the year of the book's publication, 1887, and wakes up in the year 2000, to find how much the world has changed.

Attlee's own *The Social Worker*, published in 1920, has been described by his biographer John Bew as 'the forgotten script of the twentieth-century Labour Party'. In it, he argues that the Great War had shown that everyone was involved in the life of the nation. Attlee blamed the Victorians for destroying notions of citizenship (a key concept in the 1945 Socialist Programme) and replacing it with class- or individual interest. Citizenship gave us rights but also entailed duties, to rein in self-interest at certain times and work for the general good. This mindset came naturally during a war – but, he argued, was also the correct one for peace. In another book, *The Labour Party in Perspective* (1937), he laid out much of the agenda that would be followed post 1945.

However, the most powerful Sacred Text for 1945 Socialism was created after the Programme had achieved its First Taste of Power – and not even by a socialist. The Beveridge Report came out in December 1942 (a fortnight after the Battle of El Alamein, Britain's first victory in the War and arguably the turning point of the entire conflict). Its author was a Liberal economist. The report, officially titled *Social Insurance and Allied Services,* talked of 'Five Giants on the road to reconstruction': Want, Disease, Ignorance, Squalour and Idleness. It argued that these should be fought with state-driven programmes. There should be benefits for those unable to work (including a larger old-age pension), free healthcare and education for all, a massive house-building programme and a commitment to full employment. Much more than Attlee's books, the report fired the public imagination – 600,000 copies were sold – and swung opinion behind the party determined to put its recommendations into practice, Labour.

But back to the 1930s… At that decade advanced, Hitler and Mussolini became more and more aggressive. Attlee found his feet as a Leader in response to this. Labour, and Attlee himself, had wavered on the subject of rearmament, but after a visit to Spain in December 1937, where he met, amongst others, the members of the Major Attlee Brigade, the Leader set a clear anti-appeasement tone. At times, he spoke louder and clearer than Churchill.

Britain went to war in September 1939. A 'phoney war' followed, but in April 1940, Hitler invaded Denmark and Norway. The resulting crisis created the First Taste of Power for the new Programme, as a coalition replaced the old administration. As often with First Tastes, this only came about by a close margin. Right up to, and arguably even after, the crucial 'Norway' parliamentary debate from May 7th to the 9th (best remembered for Leo Amery's telling Chamberlain "In the name of God, go" but where the major critical speech was made by Attlee), commentators expected the Chamberlain government to survive, despite the fact it was clearly limping along.

It didn't survive, of course. On the morning of May 10th, German troops flooded into the Netherlands and Belgium. Chamberlain resigned that evening. The new coalition was not led by Attlee but by Churchill. Churchill, with his pugnacity and superb oratory, was the man to lead the country. But he led it along a route that Attlee and his supporters had designed.

Most modern Churchillians will be horrified by the thought that their hero has anything to do with the most left-wing Political Programme the UK has ever seen. Culturally, his world of aristocratic privilege (and some of his expressed views on race) was the antithesis of everything that Labour stood for. But in practice, the government that he led ran wartime Britain as a highly centralized command economy. Arguably it had no option to do otherwise, but that is what it did. Attlee was Churchill's second-in-command (he moved into 11 Downing Street). The administration had men of the left (plus the occasional woman) at the highest levels. A David Low cartoon of the time, *All behind you, Winston,* shows Churchill rolling up his sleeves and marching to war. Directly behind him are not Tories but senior members of the Labour Party: Attlee, Ernest Bevin and Herbert Morrison. Attlee often deputized for Churchill in parliament, including to announce the Emergency Powers Defence Bill, which gave sweeping powers to the government of a kind more like Soviet Russia than the lost, tranquil Britain of Stanley Baldwin.

The new era's culture was communal, too. Its Archetypes were not Tranquillity's slightly amateurish gentlemen and ladies but ordinary men and women doing the fighting or working, hard, in the factories or on the land. The movie *In Which we Serve*, made about a ship and its crew in 1942, featured an aristocratic captain based on Louis Mountbatten, but all the other protagonists, such as Ordinary Seaman 'Shorty' Blake, were from other ranks. There was not a middle-ranking gent in sight.

The era's Villains, apart from Hitler and his gang, were 'spivs', who played the situation for personal profit, and the old, largely aristocratic, appeasers, the latter ripped to shreds in *Guilty Men*. This book was classic Triumphalism, as was a campaign led by Lord Beaverbrook to requisition the ornamental gates presented to the old ironmaster, Baldwin, on his retirement, and have them melted down for the war effort.

I shan't go into the specific history of the Second World War here, as it is well known. Its end, naturally, was greeted with public jubilation. The celebrations were largely classless – hadn't we all won the War together? VE Day has to be the Programme's Crowning Glory. Early, perhaps, in parliamentary terms, but bang in tune with the Zeitgeist which would soon sweep Attlee to power.

Most Conservatives didn't get this. They thought that the wartime coalition and its collectivist tone and policies were simply a temporary matter, driven by necessity. After the War, things would get back to normal, with a grateful nation voting for its warrior leader, the way it had done for Lloyd George in December 1918. This is typical 'This won't last' thinking by an old guard during a new Programme's First Taste.

Instead, the nation voted for the political Models and Values that had won the War, not the individual. It did so decisively: Labour scored a Landslide victory in the election of July 1945, a majority of 145. This was the Great Endorsement of Attlee's Programme.

In the same month, JB Priestley's *An Inspector Calls* was premiered, a classic Cultural Endorsement of the Programme's values. In it, a mysterious Inspector Goole quizzes a successful industrialist and his family about the suicide of a young working-class woman. They all turn out, in different ways, to have been responsible for her downfall. (The play is set in 1912, but the audience would have had the 1930s clearly in their minds.)

The Programme, now in its Pomp, had a number of remarkable Big Wins. Attlee's own personal favourite was the National Insurance Act of 1946, under which everyone was guaranteed unemployment- and sickness benefits and an old-age pension from age 65 for men and 60 for women, in return for paying a weekly 'stamp'. The same year saw the National Health Service Act, which mandated the Minister for Health, Nye Bevan, to set up the NHS. (Bevan finally achieved this in July 1948 – in the teeth of fierce opposition from the medical establishment: this was the Big Battle for the Programme.) 1946 also saw the New Towns Act, setting a massive, planned building programme in motion. In addition, Labour carried through its nationalization of the 'commanding heights of the economy': coal, electricity and the railways, which were all in public ownership by the end of 1947. Overseas, most of Britain's Asian Empire was dismantled.

The Programme had its First Big Failure in the winter of 1946/7. From late January to mid-March 1947 the country lay under deep snow. Power cuts were frequent, mainly due to shortages of coal. The Minister of Power, Emmanuel Shinwell, had run stocks down in late '46, not wishing to alienate those core Programme Heroes, miners, by asking them to increase production. He had done so in the hope of a mild winter...

Slow Stranglers began to attack the Programme. One was financial, the leaching away of Britain's reserves of gold and dollars. There were two big crises, one in mid-1947 and another in September 1949. In the second of these, sterling was devalued from over $4 to $2.80. This was felt as a blow to national pride and identity. We'd won the War, but look what was happening to our currency...

Another was the age and fitness of the Programme's leaders. By 1950 they were suffering from ill health and not physically up to the demanding business of governing.

A third was a dilemma caused by global events running ahead of the Programme. With the outbreak of the Korean War in June 1950, the administration found itself helplessly pinned between a desire to participate and thus support both the UN (in which Attlee believed passionately) and America (which was effectively bankrolling the UK at that time), and the desperate need not to spend scarce money on what would be an expensive conflict.

For the voters, however, what Slowly Strangled 1945 Socialism was the continuation of rationing. This lasted throughout the Programme's Pomp. Some items, like bread, were only rationed *after* the War. When Labour finally lost office in late 1951, the following items were still on the list: bacon, ham, other meat (controlled more strictly than it had been in 1945), butter, margarine, cooking fat, cheese, sugar, sweets, chocolate and tea. Rationing lasted longer after the war than during it.

The tone that went with it didn't help. At the start of 1948, a billboard went up around the country, showing Attlee and a slogan: "Let us all put into our work the spirit that has made this nation great. An all-out effort will increase our production by the 10% we need to turn the tide." John Bew points out that George Orwell's *1984* appeared soon after. Big Brother – or, rather, Uncle Clem – is watching you!

However, to core supporters of the 1945 Programme, both rationing and the billboard were perfectly reasonable. If there was a shortage of food, then whatever food there was should be shared out equally. Wasn't rationing just another part of economic planning? And as for the tone, well, citizens had duties. Good thing to remind them of it from time to time! Both rationing and the billboard flowed naturally from the Programme and its Worldview, just as ignoring a posturing overseas dictator had been the natural thing for 'Mr Tranquillity' to have done a decade earlier. Such is the nature of Political Programmes.

Beyond the party faithful, more and more voters were getting fed up with having basics rationed and being told to work 10% harder. The Conservatives played on this in the 1950 election, and slashed Attlee's majority from 146 to 5. Women, in particular, swapped allegiance. Governing with such a small majority was never going to be easy.

A Big Split then opened up in the party. In April 1951, the administration proposed saving money on the booming (and ever more costly) NHS by charging for prescriptions and for dental and optical work. Nye Bevan resigned over the issue, as did a junior minister called Harold Wilson. Cue years of bickering between supporters of Bevan and those of at first

Attlee and then the man who became his successor, Hugh Gaitskell.

Of all the Programmes in this story, this one needs the 'Body-blow' concept least. 1945 Socialism didn't so much get one Body-blow as a series of blows, each of which hurt. If there was a Body-blow to the Programme, it was probably the Split. Maybe also the death of Attlee's faithful Foil, Ernest Bevin. This was particularly upsetting for Attlee, as the two had not parted on good terms. Attlee had had to replace Bevin as Foreign Secretary as Bevin was no longer fit enough to do the job. Bevin had resented this and made his feelings clear. Attlee himself fell ill around the same time.

A second election was called for October of that year. The Conservatives gained an overall majority of 17 – their First Taste of Power. Typical of supporters of a Programme that has been newly Dethroned, former Chancellor Hugh Dalton predicted that the new government would soon hit economic and social problems and be out of office again. He was, of course, wrong.

1945 Socialism

Crucible Group: At LSE, post-1931

Leader: Clement Attlee

Core Policies: Welfare State, nationalize key industries, full employment, dismantle the Asian Empire

Carried Forward: Patriotism, respect for many traditional institutions (especially the monarchy)

Sacred Texts: *The Social Worker* (1920), Beveridge Report (1942)

Archetype: Ordinary working man (and woman)

Villains: Capitalists, spivs, old aristocratic appeasers

Gaining Significant Influence: Attlee appointed party leader, 1935

First Taste of Power: Attlee enters coalition, May 10th, 1940

Crowning Glory: VE day

Great Endorsement: 1945 election, 146 majority

Cultural Endorsement: JB Priestley, *An Inspector Calls*

Counterblast: Evelyn Waugh, *Brideshead Revisited*

Big Wins: National Insurance Act, 1946; New Towns Act, 1946; creation of NHS, 1946 – 8; nationalization of coal, electricity and railways; Indian independence

Big Battle: Bevan vs. the BMA

The First Big Failure: 1946/7 power shortage

Slow Stranglers: Financial crises; age/health of leaders; financial implications of the Korean War; continuation of rationing and the hectoring tone that went with it

Big Split: Bevanite rebellion over NHS charges

Dethronement: Conservative victory of 1951

Waterloo: Conservative Landslide of 1955

Fifties 'One Nation' Conservatism, 1951 - 1964

A number of younger Conservatives had been promoted to positions of responsibility in the Churchill/Attlee Coalition. 'Rab' Butler, then aged thirty-eight, was given a Cabinet post in 1941 and went on to create the 1944 Education Act, which provided free education for all. Harold Macmillan, author of a 1938 book called *The Middle Way* which advocated economic planning and a minimum wage, received a Cabinet post in 1942. While Conservative in asserting the existing social order and drawing their support mainly from the middle and upper classes, these rising stars on the left of the party remembered the Jarrow marches and were keen to protect the working classes against the more extreme consequences of *laissez faire* Capitalism (a system they referred to as 'devil-take-the-hindmost').

Looking back, the appointments of Butler and Macmillan can be seen as moments when Significant Influence was achieved by a still Aspirant Political Programme.

In May 1947, the party published a pamphlet called *The Industrial Charter*, which suggested moving with times and accepting most of the Beveridge reforms. Macmillan, one of its authors, talked of 'the impossibility of unscrambling those scrambled eggs.' It would become a Sacred Text of the new Programme.

However, when it was debated at that year's Party Conference, the Charter proved controversial. Churchill, now no longer having to run a wartime economy, was not impressed. Old-school Tory Sir Waldron

Smithers denounced it as 'milk and water socialism'. New Programmes often face strong internal opposition to start with.

It took another election – that of February 1950 – and a large input of younger MPs to really get change moving. Nine of these new arrivals quickly formed a group called 'One Nation'. This was a classic Crucible Group, meeting over dinner – no doubt at a venue that had found a way round meat rationing – and discussing their vision for what would soon become a new Political Programme. The group included Edward Heath, Iain Macleod, Angus Maude and Enoch Powell, all men who had fought in the War – as officers, of course: Shorty Blake would have had trouble selecting the right cutlery and might have passed the port in the wrong direction.

In the same year, the group published a pamphlet that bore its name, *One Nation*. In it, they argued that the Welfare State should be maintained but made to work more efficiently (a classic way of reframing the carrying forward of popular opposition policies). Rather than serve everyone, the welfare system should be a safety net, providing 'a minimum standard, above which people should be free to rise as far as their industry, their thrift, their ability or their genius may take them'. Alongside the provision of this net, the government's job was to defend the nation, keep the currency sound and tax people as little as possible. It was not responsible for creating equality.

The group would continue to issue influential pamphlets during the 1950s.

The Programme won its First Taste of Power quickly, in the October 1951 election. This was a classic First Taste: very provisional. The Tories actually got fewer votes than Labour but won more seats. This was partially because of constituency boundaries, some seats being more populous than others, but also because Labour had huge majorities in its stronghold seats, while the majorities in many Conservative ones (especially the newly-won ones) were small. But that was the system, and the 1945 Programme was duly dethroned.

The win also reflected the changing mood of the time. The new Programme would go on to have its Great Endorsement at the next election, in May 1955, where it won a majority of 60 seats and received 49.7% of the votes – a percentage it has never achieved again since, not even in the Thatcher years.

As they said they would, the new power-holders carried forward much of the old 1945 Socialist reforms, especially those inspired by Beveridge. Some historians argue that the new government kept so much of the old Programme that there was no real change of Political Programme at this time. They talk instead of 'Butskellism' (a made-up name from the Tory and Labour chancellors, Rab Butler and Hugh Gaitskell) and of a 'post-war consensus' that lasted from 1945 to 1979.

However, new Programmes always carry forward some aspects of the old. And 1951 saw real changes in policy direction. Nationalization was halted. Iron and steel companies, bar one, were put back in private hands. The market was prioritized over central planning. The ending of rationing, as soon as possible, was made a priority. But even these clear differences were not the key divide between the two Programmes. That was cultural.

There were no more billboards exhorting people to produce 10% more: in the new Programme's Britain, billboards would be for advertising washing machines or TVs. Gone was the working man as Archetype, busy at the coalface or shovelling the coal into the boiler of a locomotive. Now the narrative was about the middle-class family enjoying their head-earned leisure, sitting down to their unrationed traditional British Sunday roast – cooked, of course, by the proud wife, though the equally proud husband did the decent thing afterwards and helped with the washing up, while their son played with his Meccano and their daughter with her dolls. We were no longer Attleean 'citizens' but subjects of the King, and, after February 1952, a beautiful young Queen.

Were the workers dumped, then? No. The Conservatives have always been too astute to do that, with a long tradition, from Disraeli through Churchill's father, Lord Randolph, and Churchill himself, of 'Tory Democracy'. The working class was no longer encouraged to proudly contemplate its existing virtues, as it had been by Labour, but asked to stay patriotic and to better itself economically. The wherewithal to do the latter – new consumer goods – became more and more available as the 1950s continued. The far left saw this as pernicious *embourgeoisement*, the erosion of sacred class identity. Workers and their families, by and large, simply enjoyed the new stuff. "Most of our people have never had it so good," crowed the Programme's ultimate leader, Macmillan, in a speech in 1957.

He really did mean 'most' and would love to have said 'all'. He also meant 'our': like those tranquil Baldwinites, Fifties Conservatives were paternalist. They believed in deference to the old order and its representatives. There was a Salisburian sense that this order was something sacred, which had evolved over centuries and had made our nation great. Liberal intellectuals and socialists who criticized or mocked it were 'too clever by half'. Macmillan wrote in his diary how much he hated holidays where there were 'masses of tourists' but loved the moors where he went shooting, where 'the hills, the keepers, the farmers, the farmers' sons, the drivers… always remined the same'.

The era tuned into radio programmes like 'Two Way Family Favourites', with Doris Day telling us in 1956 that whatever would be, would be, or (for my generation) 'Children's Favourites', with its emblematic theme tune *Puffin' Billy* played by the Melodi Light Orchestra. From 1955, the televised streets of Dock Green were patrolled by the avuncular PC George Dixon. In the theatre, there was the gentle humour of Flanders and Swann or Terrence Rattigan's moral dilemmas of the upper middle class. The standard high culture menu featured Dickens, Shakespeare and classical music (including sitting with a pained look through something, hopefully brief, by Hindemith or Bartók, to show you could be 'modern', too).

The War, of course, continued to cast a long shadow over the era's culture. But it was presented in a different way. It hadn't been won by Shorty Blake after all, but by daring young bucks, often played by Kenneth More. This Programme's war heroes were dashing and, after all, gentlemanly.

There was a flip side to all this apparent lightness: an insistence on conformity. A certain amount of youthful exuberance was fine, especially for chaps, but there were boundaries. If you found yourself outside these, you were in trouble.

The Villains of the Fifties Conservative culture were 'the Russians' and bolshy trade unionists intent on perpetuating a now-outdated class war. But the Villain-making also seeped into the (by many people) strongly-held prejudices of the era, particularly homophobia.

Homophobia was linked to worries about security, as it was felt that gay men, in particular, could be targets for blackmail. (The idea that you could change this by simply accepting gay people didn't occur to Fifties Conservatives.) But there was something more visceral to the prejudice than this. The Fifties seem to be an era of particularly virulent homophobia – maybe the era's 'all in it together' culture needed some extra 'others' to define itself against.

The most notable victim was Alan Turing, but many more people suffered. At the end of 1954, there were over 1000 men in prison for committing homosexual acts. A number of them had been caught in entrapment exercises set up by the police. In the same year, the Home Secretary, David Maxwell-Fyfe, who once described homosexuality as a 'plague', ordered an official report on the issue. One must assume that he hoped it would advocate taking a firmer line, but when the Wolfenden Report came out, in September 1957, it favoured liberalization. Maxwell-Fyfe, by then in the Lords, voted against it. The recommendations weren't implemented.

Racial prejudice was also a feature of 1950s life, occasionally erupting into violence, but the Programme didn't play that card, unlike their active homophobia (and unlike some Conservatives in the 1960s). However, they did quietly allow a 'colour bar', whereby non-whites could not get any kind of supervisory position, to exist in many workplaces. The one at Euston station was not ended until 1966.

The Programme's insistence on uniformity spilled over into censorship, which was tightened in the early 1950s. In 1954, Donald McGill's saucy seaside postcards were banned from a number of resorts. Magistrates in Swindon ordered the destruction of a translation of Boccaccio's *Decameron* in a local bookshop. Later on, in 1960, the establishment would attempt to prevent publication of DH Lawrence's erotic novella *Lady Chatterley's Lover*, which, according to the leading barrister for the Crown, was not something you would wish 'your wife or your servants' to read.

There was, of course, a Counterblast. John Osborne's *Look Back in Anger* premiered at the Royal Court Theatre in May 1956, its twenty-something hero furious about the class system and what he sees as the stifling smugness of the era. The Angry Young Men had arrived.

However, many more young men – and women – were having fun rather than getting angry. Top of the UK charts in November 1955 was *Rock Around the Clock* by Bill Haley and His Comets. In 1957, Elvis Presley (or his music, anyway) really hit the UK, with his first UK Number One, *All Shook Up*. Rock'n'roll wasn't so much a Counterblast to Fifties Conservatism as a message from an alternative universe that completely ignored it. The new popular culture faltered after Elvis was drafted into the US Army, but would come back, even more vibrant, in the next decade, ready to chime culturally with the Programme's successor and be skilfully corralled into the political arena by it.

The Programme's Great Escape was the Suez Crisis of 1956. Egyptian President Gamal Abdel Nasser nationalized the strategically essential canal in July of that year. Britain and another nation smarting from diminution of Empire, France, decided to grab it back (with some help from Israel) by military force. Their operation began successfully, but the rest of the world rounded on them and they were forced to abandon it.

This was a national humiliation. However, the Programme did not collapse after it, despite talk to that effect around the time. Many old-school patriot voters had supported the action. When a *post mortem* debate on Suez was conducted in parliament in 1957, the government had a big

112

enough majority to survive, despite a few defections. Radical opponents crowed at the establishment's embarrassment and fumed at the result of the parliamentary debate; a few careers (including that of PM Anthony Eden) suffered; but otherwise little changed.

In fact, the Programme gained momentum. Eden was replaced by a more effective leader, Harold Macmillan, who would keep the job for nearly seven years. The period has gone down in history as 'the Macmillan era'. With its proper Leader now in place, the Programme had a real Pomp. The economy grew. The administration steered the nation (and the world) through the geopolitical crises of the Berlin Wall and Cuba crises of 1961/2. Macmillan played his diplomatic cards skilfully, and ended up a co-signatory to a treaty banning the testing of the nuclear weapons that had, at one point, seemed to threaten the entire life of the planet.

However Slow Stranglers began to emerge.

Taxation remained stubbornly high. This had not been the original intention of the Programme, but the twin costs of keeping a Welfare system going at home and a global military presence abroad were just too high. The nation was living beyond its means.

Inflation began to threaten. 1961 saw it double from 2.2% to 4.4%.

More generally, there was a growing sense of economic underperformance. Britain might never have had it so good, but across the Channel, European countries were having it even better. Germany was booming – its GDP had actually overtaken ours. France and Italy were growing faster than us, too. An attempt to boost our economic performance, 'National Productivity Year', was launched in November 1962, but achieved little. A set of stamps issued to celebrate the campaign became notorious for printing errors.

Macmillan became determined to get Britain into what was then called the EEC, the European club of France, Germany, Benelux and Italy. Long negotiations were carried out – but in the end, these all hit the brick wall of General de Gaulle. The General's "Non!", announced at a press conference in January 1963, was a public relations disaster for the Programme. This was its First Big Failure. As it was essentially foreign policy, it did not hurt British citizens directly. But rejection dented the confidence of the administration.

The Body-blow came shortly afterwards, as the Profumo Affair unfolded over 1963. John Profumo, Secretary of State for War in the cabinet, had an affair with Christine Keeler, a teenage (when they met) model whose other lovers included a Russian spy. This, in itself, appalled more strait-laced party supporters, including Macmillan. But Profumo then lied about it in the House of Commons, threatening libel suits for anyone who raised the issue again, before finally admitting the truth.

Fifties' Conservatism had been built on the belief that the old class system worked. The people at the top might have privilege, but they strove for the common, national good and kept to the same conventional personal rules as everyone else. The Profumo Affair destroyed that story, and with it a key prop of the Programme.

Macmillan's health declined sharply after, and forced him to retire on the eve of that year's Party Conference, in October. Who should the Conservatives get to replace him? A new mood of youth and optimism was emerging – instantiated by the election, in November 1960, of John F Kennedy as US president. The Conservatives needed to do the same: pick someone young, dynamic, upwardly mobile.

The party grandees chose the sixty-year-old 14th Earl of Home, a man so patrician that you had to come from the right side of the tracks to know how to pronounce his name properly (one said "Hume").

Despite this, and an admission that he 'did his economics with matchsticks', Home was not the upper-class twit that his detractors gleefully presented him as. He was intelligent, likeable and conscientious. But his selection sent out totally the wrong message to a country that was now eager for change. The old Programme was limping along and would soon be put out of its misery.

Fifties 'One Nation' Conservatism

Leader: Harold Macmillan

Replacement Leader: Sir Alec Douglas-Home

Core Policies: Mixed economy

Carried forward: Beveridge 'safety net'

Crucible Group: 'One Nation' dining club

Sacred Texts: *The Middle Way* (1938), *The Industrial Charter* (1947), *One Nation* (1950)

Archetype: The middle-class family

Villains: The Russians, old-fashioned class warriors, (for some) homosexuals

Bright Future: Old social order; new prosperity for all

Gaining Significant Influence: Butler and Macmillan join wartime Cabinet

First Taste of Power: Narrow victory of 1951

Great Endorsement: 60-seat victory in 1955

Crowning Glory: Coronation / Ascent of Everest

Cultural Endorsement: *'Que sera, sera', Dixon of Dock Green,* Flanders and Swann, the plays of Terrence Rattigan

Cultural Counterblast: *Look Back in Anger*

Big Wins: Removal of rationing, 'Never had it so good', test ban treaty

Great Escape: Suez Crisis

First Big Failure: Rejected application to join EEC

Slow Stranglers: Poor economic performance relative to Europe, rising inflation

Body-blow: Profumo Affair

Dethronement: Labour victory of 1964

Waterloo: Labour victory of 1966

'White Heat' Modernization, 1964 - 1970

A radically different Programme, way more in tune with the new temper of the new decade, was waiting in the wings. As usual, it first got its First Taste of Power, winning the election held in October 1964, by a tiny majority: 4. But that was enough.

The Big Idea of the Programme was modernization. Its Leader was Harold Wilson, though its lasting achievements would turn out to be those of his Foil, Roy Jenkins, Home Secretary from 1965 to 1967.

Wilson is often presented as an opportunist. Though he could be one at times, he was much a more serious thinker than that. He moved on from participating in internal party squabbles to creating a new Big Idea, with clear, fresh Models, Values and Stories. Wilson wasn't just 'a Bevanite' or 'a Gaitskellite'; he was the creator of a new Political Programme.

The son of an industrial chemist, he believed passionately in technology, planning, and the ability of these to change society. These ideas were nurtured in a Crucible Group which began meeting at the Reform Club in the 1950s. Led by left-leaning Nobel Prize winning physicist Patrick Blackett, it included leading scientists and writers (including the then influential CP Snow) – and some Labour politicians, especially Wilson.

Wilson didn't create his Big Idea because he spotted a gap in the political marketplace, he did so because he believed in it.

The new ideas were set out in a policy document that can be seen as the

Sacred Text of Wilsonism, *Signposts for the Sixties*, which he co-authored in 1960. But the new Big Idea was most forcefully expressed in Wilson's Party Conference speech at Scarborough in October 1963, when he inspired his audience with his vision of a technology-driven society. There would be 'planning on an unprecedented scale to meet automation without unemployment; a pooling of talent in which all classes could compete and prosper; a vast extension of state-sponsored research; a completely new concept of education; an alliance of science and socialism.' A new Britain was going to be 'forged' in the 'white heat' of this revolution.

The people doing this forging would be very different from the drivers of the old Programme, those old, languid, southern, C of E, educated-in-Classics-at-public-school, had-a-good-War Fifties Conservatives. Wilson was a generation younger than Macmillan, and grammar-school educated. His background was Northern and Nonconformist. He was hard-working, a meritocrat (in the non-ironic sense of the word). CP Snow entitled one of his novels, which bemoaned the downplaying of science in our culture, 'The New Men'. Wilson was one of these.

Snow's novels were popular among the intelligentsia, but the Cultural Endorsement of the Programme was much wider. Over 80% of UK households now owned TV sets, and viewers could watch the satire of programmes like *That Was The Week That Was*, or the street realism of *Z Cars*, a police series that depicted realistic Liverpudlian policemen in their shiny new Ford Zephyrs. *The Wednesday Play*, which ran for the whole time of the Programme, looked critically at social issues, and featured top-quality works like *Cathy Come Home*, *Up the Junction* and Denis Potter's *Nigel Barton* miniseries.

And then there were The Beatles… Wilson was not a fan – he much preferred Gilbert and Sullivan – but he knew how to harness their popularity. The Fab Four were misfits in the old order but godsends to the new one. They were working class, but had no intention of being defined by their roots (Lennon's *Working Class Hero* wasn't written until 1970). Instead, they became something class-transcendent, superstars, and created the music by which the people set free by the new Programme celebrated their lives. They also enjoyed a good laugh at the new Villains, the supporters of the old Programme – watch the train sequence in the film *A Hard Day's Night*.

A second election, in March 1966, gave the Programme its Great Endorsement, 98 seats worth. This was followed, on 30th July, by its Crowning Glory (south of Hadrian's Wall and east of Offa's Dyke, anyway), when England won the football World Cup.

However, beneath these appearances, trouble was already brewing. Wilson's planned economic changes were not proving as effective as had been hoped. He had created a new Department of Economic Affairs in 1964. This was supposed to be a rival to the economically cautious Treasury: its brief was bold economic planning. However, from the start, reality kept on refusing to fit in with the DEA's plans.

Two particularly pesky refuseniks were international currency traders (demonized in the Programme's Stories as 'the gnomes of Zurich') and the domestic trade unions. A strong pound was part of the plan (it also signalled national pride and confidence). But Britain was importing more than it was exporting, which put the pound under perpetual pressure. A strike in 1966 by the National Union of Seamen, who wanted a bigger pay rise than the planners allowed, intensified this. Money was required to prop up the currency, so cuts had to be made elsewhere.

Wilson found himself caught between two options: formally devalue the pound, or make spending cuts that would effectively mean the end of the grand economic plan. Historians now all seem to agree that he should have taken the former route. Spooked by memories of 1949, he took the latter.

In terms of the model proposed in this book, this meant a U-turn, diverging from the Core Policies of his Programme, which were designed to build a rationally-planned, technology-driven economy initially supported by government expenditure.

Luckily for the Programme, it had another aspect to its Big Idea. If Wilson wanted to modernize the economy, his Foil, Roy Jenkins, wanted to modernize our values and lifestyles. When Jenkins became Home Secretary, he was the youngest person to hold the job since Winston Churchill back in 1910. It showed. The Beatles, who never wrote any songs about five-year plans or Magnox reactors, were much better allies for him than for Wilson. Both Jenkins and John Lennon understood the deep need for the freedom to express oneself by living an intense cultural and emotional life. (Jenkins was hardly a fan, however. There are no swinging sixties tracks in the music he later chose for Desert Island Discs, where the only modern piece is Vangelis' *Chariots of Fire*.)

Jenkins' part of the Programme had been trailed in two Sacred Texts. Anthony Crosland's *The Future of Socialism* was published in 1956. Crosland, a *bon viveur*, wanted above all for everyone to have the same opportunities for good living as he had. Criticizing the rather drab world of Attleean citizenship, he wanted Britain to be 'a more colourful and civilized country to live in'.

In 1959, Jenkins published his own book, *The Labour Case*. He wrote: 'Let us be on the side of those who want people to be free to live their own lives, to make their own mistakes, and to decide, in an adult way and provided they do not infringe the rights of others, the code by which they wish to live; and on the side of experiment and brightness, of better buildings and better food, of better music (jazz as well as Bach) and better books, of fuller lives and greater freedom. In the long run these things will be more important than the most perfect of economic policies.'

In Jenkins' two years as Home Secretary in this Programme, bills were passed to legalize abortion, decriminalize homosexual acts, simplify the painful divorce system and abolish birching in prisons. He also initiated bills that ended up being passed once he had left the Home Office, removing the antiquated theatre censorship system and outlawing the refusal of housing, employment or public services to someone on grounds of race.

Subsequent Political Programmes have grumbled at Jenkins' reforms. Thatcherites loathed them, and even Tony Blair enjoyed the odd pop at them. No subsequent Programme has undone any of them, however, and they have become part of modern British life.

Home Secretary Jenkins was also a Wilsonian modernizer of the police, cutting the number of forces drastically, and of the court system, introducing majority verdicts in for a range of offences. Both reforms were initially resisted by the bodies in question, but have subsequently been accepted as constructive and necessary.

Jenkins' Britain became a place of cultural celebration, driven by young people, many from working class origins. The Beatles were the flagship, but there were a hundred other great bands and artists, such as musician

Ray Davies (son of a slaughterhouse worker), photographer Terry O'Neill (born in Romford)(he became famous for taking a picture of the old Programme's RA Butler asleep at Heathrow Airport) and fashion designer Mary Quant, from a Welsh mining family. *The Liverpool Scene,* a 1967 anthology featuring young Merseyside poets, was tutted at by the establishment – 'popsters and barbarians' said one critic – but sold half a million copies.

Indian and Chinese restaurants appeared on the streets of British towns and cities. Package holidays to sunnier climes became available, especially thanks to the Thomson Organization, which entered that market in 1965. The contraceptive pill was made available to unmarried women in 1967, the same year of the first colour TV broadcast (of Wimbledon on BBC2). BBC1 and ITV went colour in 1969.

If there was a Counterblast to the new culture, it was muted. Christopher Booker's *The Neophiliacs* critiqued it in 1969, but few people were listening. If there was a lively cultural alternative to Swinging London, it lay in the even more swinging 'alternative society' of drugs, ultra-left/anarchist protest and sexual experimentation, which stuck two, probably stoned, fingers up to parliamentary politics of any kind. The 'alternatives' excoriated Wilson for supporting US involvement in Vietnam – unfairly: Wilson, an Atlanticist at heart, risked alienating his most important global ally by keeping the UK out of the conflict, something that the more hip, liberal Tony Blair proved unable to do forty years later.

Meanwhile, Wilson's half of the Programme spluttered along, bedevilled by constant sterling crises. Following the 1966 one, another followed in 1967, also triggered by a strike, this time in the docks. This second crisis forced Wilson's hand: the pound had to be devalued after all. It wasn't as spectacular as 1949, but the cut from the pound's being worth \$2.80 to \$2.40, in November 1967, was still seen as humiliating. It was a Body-blow. The polls turn bright blue at that time, and show huge Tory leads for the next two years. Nobody was impressed by Wilson's speech where he told voters that 'the pound in your pocket has not been devalued'. The gnomes had won.

Wilson tried to keep his White Heat revolution going, but to little effect. Mergers between large companies, especially in the automotive, electrical and computing sectors, were encouraged by a new Industrial Reorganization Corporation. The hope was that these would create greater efficiency. They did – sometimes. A Selective Employment Tax tried to boost employment in export-based manufacturing and take it away from domestic services. It did little to boost manufacturing and damaged the service sector. In many British towns, Wilsonite planning saw modern rectangular concrete office- or accommodation blocks replacing older buildings. Some of those older buildings, no doubt, had been in need of renovation, but they had created community. The new concrete, once shiny, started looking rather shabby after a few winters of British rain.

The once-mighty flagship Department of Economic Affairs was wound up in late 1969, the Treasury quietly rubbing its hands and taking back what was left of its role. The DEA lives on as the 'Department of Administrative Affairs' in the TV sitcom *Yes Minister.*

Wilson's Big Idea of a meritocratic Britain with technology centre stage had been supremely timely. Yet its Pomp was painfully short-lived. The Programme seemed to have difficulty choosing the right Normal Politics to go with its powerful, liberating vision. Economic planning turned out to be tricky. Its failure led to a scepticism about governmental planning

123

that has lasted to this day.

Still, Wilsonism did have Big Wins. Higher education was expanded. A lasting legacy of White Heat modernization is the Open University, established in 1969. This aimed to improve the national level of education, offering degree courses to people who, having missed the academic boat as youngsters, wanted to climb on board later in life. This is still going strong.

The motorway network was developed and driving made much safer thanks to the 70mph speed limit, the introduction of the breathalyser and rules on seatbelts. This represented a major opening up of life for millions of people from Wilson's own background who suddenly found that they could afford cars. Both the new roads and the new rules were an essential part of this. For Fifties Conservatives, 'motoring' had been for the few, and tiresome rules were seen as unnecessary. As the roads expanded and filled up with the many, rules became necessary.

Housing was improved in a number of ways, with over a million new homes built, the expansion of New Towns, legislation to protect tenants against unscrupulous landlords and a scheme to help poorer people get on the property ladder.

The Wilson cabinet also featured many more women than any previous one. If the classic Great Offices of State were still held by men, the female voice was influential. Many of the transport reforms were driven by Barbara Castle. Jennie Lee was put in charge of the Open University project, one dear to Wilson's heart. (Castle was made 'First Secretary of State', a rather nebulous title similar to Deputy PM. Principled and strong-willed, she would have made a great successor to Wilson, but Britain wasn't ready for a female PM at that time.)

However, Slow Stranglers were at work. I've already mentioned the global currency markets and deteriorating industrial relations. The second of these grew ever more destructive as the sixties drew to a close, with unofficial, 'wildcat' strikes adding to the existing unwillingness of the unions to go along with the planners. During most of the decade, the number of working days lost due to strikes was under 4 million a year. In 1968, it was 4.7 million, and in 1969, it was 6.8 million.

In response to this, Labour produced a white paper called *In Place of Strife*. This proposed a number of measures, including the insistence on a ballot of all members if a union in a key industry called a strike, a 28-day cooling off period for wildcat strikes, and stiff penalties for any union that broke the new rules. The cabinet was divided over it, and it never made it onto the statute book.

The result was a slow ratcheting up of inflation, which passed 5% in 1969. Given the rates that would soon prevail, this sounds peanuts – but at the time it looked scary, not having been that high since 1952.

A third corrosive force was cultural: our loss of confidence in technology as a solution to all our problems. Even back in 1963, when Wilson gave his famous speech, the long-term damage caused to the planet by the unthinking use of technology was already being flagged up by Rachel Carson's ground-breaking *Silent Spring*. In 1967 wrecked tanker *Torrey Canyon* spilled millions of gallons of crude oil onto once-beautiful Cornish beaches, shocking many of us – especially once pictures of dying seabirds coated in oil appeared in the press. The first Tory leads in polls appear around that time. In 1968, three people were killed when a corner of one of the smart new tower-blocks, at Ronan Point in East London, collapsed two months after it had been opened.

The rising counter-culture of the era took this disillusion even further. It saw technology as an enemy of virtue. Nature was a source of beauty and spiritual strength, in need of defence against uptight, over-rational, arrogant men who sought to exploit and ruin it for selfish, short-term, material ends.

Back in the mainstream, there was something of a backlash against Jenkins' liberalizing measures. The unpleasantness of the Altamont festival in America in late 1969 belied the dream that ever more freedom was inevitably beneficial. And on April 10th, 1970, something unthinkable to the true sixties child happened: Paul announced he was quitting The Beatles.

Paul's departure had very little effect on poll data – but the romantic, cultural side of me can't help thinking that this is what took the final steam out of the Programme. It had ridden the wave of the Fab Four's success to its own cultural and political triumph. It would fall with it.

The end of the decade saw real growth in the economy. The polls began to look less terrifying. Had the nation forgiven the Programme for the devaluation of the pound, back in 1967, after all? Wilson, with the support of his cabinet, called an early election. Arguably one reason for the timing was the 1970 football World Cup, for which England were favourites. The date chosen, June 18th, was just after the semi-finals.

England never reached the semis. 2-0 up in our quarter-final against Germany at one point, we ended up losing 3-2.

The Conservative leader Ted Heath came up with a catchy Slogan, claiming he would cut prices 'at a stroke' (exactly how was never made clear, but such is the way of Slogans). Regrettably, another factor in the election was probably the playing of the race card by certain Conservative politicians, though Heath, a fundamentally decent man, did not approve. Heath won by a majority of 30.

Programme over.

'White Heat' Modernization

Leader: Harold Wilson

Foil: Roy Jenkins

Core Policies: Planned economy. Social liberalization

Crucible Group: Patrick Blackett's Reform Club group

Sacred Texts: *The Labour Case* (1959). *Signposts to the Sixties* (1960)

Archetype: Ex-grammar-school scientist/planner in white coat

Villains: Privileged elite, 'old boy network', 'gnomes of Zurich'

Bright Future: Efficient meritocracy, (Jenkins) more joyfulness

Gaining Significant Influence: Wilson becomes Party Leader, 1963

First Taste of Power: Narrow victory of 1964

Great Endorsement: Big victory in 1966

Crowning Glory: England win World Cup, 30th June 1966

Cultural Endorsements: *Z-Cars,* The Wednesday Play, The Beatles
    (and many other bands), 'Swinging London'

Cultural Counterblast: The full-on alternative society

Big Wins: Jenkins' social reforms, creation of Open University

Slow Stranglers: Currency markets, industrial unrest, inflation, loss of
    confidence in technology as a cure-all

Body-blow: Devaluation of the pound, November 1967

Dethronement: Conservative victory of 1970

Waterloo: Oil crisis of 1973/4

The 1970s: Two Aspirant Programmes
that never made it

1. Heathism

The Conservative Party had ditched Alec Douglas-Home in 1965 and appointed in his stead a leader for the new era: grammar-school alumnus and meritocrat Ted Heath. Heath, a member of the One Nation group back in 1950, didn't set up a Crucible Group – he wasn't really a group person – but did the next best thing: organize a conference to thrash out a new Action Plan for the party. This took place at the Selsdon Park Hotel, a former Victorian country house in what was by then leafy suburbia, in January 1970.

At this, Heath appeared to ditch his old one-nation caution and presided over a conference that looked to the economic right for inspiration. Less state expenditure. No more support for ailing businesses ('lame ducks') or meddling with business ownership *à la* Industrial Reorganization Corporation. No planned levels of prices and incomes. No Keynesian macroeconomic tinkering. The market would be in charge.

Wilson was dismissive, talking of 'Selsdon Man' as if the conference were a gathering of vicious prehistoric anthropoids (in fact, the delegates were ahead of their time). But Heath's party won the election that followed that summer. Its majority was not a Great Endorsement, but it was a decent First Taste of Power for the new Aspirant Programme.

Some of the old Programme was carried forward into the new. There was a Wilsonian technocratic feel to Heathism. Efficiency remained a watchword. Some old counties were replaced by efficient (in theory) new ones. The old currency of pounds, shillings and pence was decimalized (a Labour policy, but it could have been cancelled).

The new Programme soon got into trouble. The Selsdon agenda proved impossible to realize. In 1971, the government bailed out Rolls Royce, which had encountered cost overruns on its new RB211 aero engine. This was a wise move, as the engine would go on to be a huge success, but it was a major U-turn. In the same year, Upper Clyde Shipbuilders went bankrupt. The government refused to bail it out – and its shop stewards organized a 'work-in'. Cue another U-turn when the embarrassed government finally stepped in after all.

Meanwhile, unemployment had begun to rise. Heath's new Chancellor, Anthony Barber, tried to counteract this with a 'dash for growth' involving tax cuts financed by government borrowing. A target of 10% growth was plucked out of the air as an aim.

This was a disaster. Inflation, which had dipped during 1971/2, giving the illusion that it was back under control, began to rise again, and this time it kept rising. So much for 'cutting prices at a stroke'. Unions began competing in a game of 'ask for the biggest pay rise'. This resulted in yet another U-turn, the creation of a Prices and Incomes policy, which the unions simply ignored.

All hell broke loose, with inflation soaring, strikes hitting levels not seen since 1926 and, ultimately, industry being forced to work a three-day week. The UK stock market went into a slow but relentless freefall: the crash of 1973/4 was worse than anything from the 1930s, with the FT index losing an astonishing 73% of its value.

One can argue that circumstances were against Heath. He was unlucky in a personal way. His most able supporter, his chancellor Ian Macleod, died a few weeks after the victory. Macleod would have been less likely to launch Barber's disastrous dash. He was unlucky geopolitically, too. The 1973/4 oil crisis occurred on his watch. But above all, he was unlucky because the time simply wasn't right for him. It would take the 'Winter of Discontent', at the other end of the decade, to change the mood of the nation to one that would accept the Thatcherite view of trade union power.

However, Heath also made big mistakes. He came up with an Aspirant Programme, convinced the electorate of it, then dumped a large chunk of it. He was a fair-weather Selsdonian, but Political Programme Leaders cannot be fair-weather. Whatever the rights and wrongs of their Programme, once they have placed themselves at the head of it, they must remain loyal to its Big Idea, Worldview and Core Policies. The Enoch Powell quote I cited earlier, about the dangers of 'seeking to govern in direct opposition to the principles with which [an administration has been] entrusted with the right to govern', dates from this era.

However, there was another aspect to 'Heathism', and here Heath stuck to his guns and the Programme succeeded. Heath believed passionately that Britain should join the European Communities (a.k.a. the 'Common Market'). It was part of his 1970 manifesto, and on 1st January 1973, the UK, along with Denmark and Ireland, joined. A Big Win.

However, too many Core Policies had been ditched. In the face of a miners' strike in February 1974, Heath called an election on the simple question: 'Who governs Britain?'

131

'Not you,' the electorate replied, though it couldn't really decide who did. (We had been undecided through the entire period of Heathism, with no party getting any real lead in the polls for any real length of time.)

No party emerged with an overall majority, though Harold Wilson had four more seats than Heath. After a few days trying to form alliances with smaller parties, Heath quit Number Ten. His Programme never got a Great Endorsement.

Heathism: Selsdon and Europe

Leader: Ted Heath

Big Idea: Power of the free market – within Europe

Carried forward: Meritocracy, focus on efficiency

Gaining Significant Influence: Heath becomes Party Leader in 1965

Crucible Group: Conference at Selsdon Park Hotel

First Taste of Power: Election victory of 1970

Great Endorsement: *not achieved*

Big Win: Joining EC in 1973

First Big Failure: Series of U-turns

Slow Stranglers: Deteriorating industrial relations, relentless fall of
stock market

Body-blow: Miners' strike begins, 5th February 1974

Dethronement: Loses majority in 28th February 1974 election

Waterloo: Labour election victory, November 1974

---

2. The Social Contract

A Labour government took power instead, initially as a minority, but, after a second election in November 1974, with a majority, albeit a tiny one. The springboard to a Great Endorsement later? Time would tell.

Harold Wilson was still party Leader, but this was Wilson Mark 2. The events and the new Zeitgeist of the early 1970s had destroyed the appeal of White Heat. Instead, the new Aspirant Political Programme had a new Big Idea, the Social Contract. This was essentially a deal between the Labour Party and the unions. Labour would put in place a set of policies of which the unions approved, and in return the unions would moderate their pay demands.

It was not a bad idea in theory. The German economy had been based on such a deal for decades. However, it didn't work here. Neither side kept to the bargain. I suspect that the leaders of the larger unions meant to keep to it, but they proved incapable of controlling their more militant shop-stewards. The government didn't help by cutting public expenditure – a U-turn, though arguably unavoidable given the state of the economy, which soon became parlous.

A sense began to grow, that the UK had somehow become ungovernable. In 1975, former SAS hero David Stirling set up a group of ex-military men called Great Britain 75, ready to take over if the country collapsed into anarchy.

There was no real Cultural Endorsement of the new Programme – arguably because it never really stood for anything very interesting. The song *Part of the Union* by Strawbs was an attempt to send up the overpowerful union movement, but that movement cleverly appropriated it. More attention-grabbing was the raucous Counterblast of punk, which emerged in 1976. While hardly music to Tory ears, there was something proto-Thatcherite about its insistence on individual freedom. Punks and entrepreneurs do it their way.

Wilson retired in 1976, shortly after his 60th birthday. He was replaced by Jim Callaghan, a classic Replacement Leader, solid and decent – he was one of the Queen's favourite PMs – but not driven to power on the crest of a rising Zeitgeist, the way Wilson had been back in 1964. Soon after, the Gallup polling organization asked Britons who they thought was the most powerful man in the country. The answer was Jack Jones, General Secretary of the Transport and General Workers' Union.

1976 also saw the First Big Failure of the Programme, when the government had to approach the International Monetary Fund for a loan (the money actually came through in early 1977). This came at the price of watering down the Programme's social legislation. Though this did not go down well in the polls, ratings did recover. The decision hurt the Programme, but was not fatal to it.

The 'Winter of Discontent' of 1978/1979 *was* fatal, a classic, crippling Body-blow. There were strikes by lorry drivers, railwaymen, NHS workers, refuse collectors and, most emblematic, gravediggers. Many of these strikes were wildcat, called by individual shop stewards eager to carve out a reputation for militancy. Britain being Britain, the weather also took a hand, with blizzards on New Year's Eve, the coldest January since 1963 and no real let-up till late February. (My left-wing friends insist that the 'Winter of Discontent' narrative was a product of right-wing media. Yes, the term itself was first used to describe the era by the *Sun* newspaper, but I remember walking through Central London streets full of stinking rubbish piled up in corners, and sensing that things had got terminally out of hand, in a way I had not experienced before. Maybe our nose is our most sensitive political organ.)

The Social Contract

Leader: Harold Wilson (Mark 2)

Replacement Leader: Jim Callaghan

Carried forward: Attempts at Prices and Incomes policies

First Taste of Power: Largest party after election of 1974

Great Endorsement: *not achieved*

Cultural Endorsement: *not much*

Counterblast: *My Way*, Sid Vicious

First Big Failure: Cash handout from International Monetary Fund, 1976/7

Slow Strangler: Industrial relations

Body-blow: Winter of Discontent, 1978/9

Dethronement: Conservative victory of 1979

Waterloo: 1980 Labour Party Conference

Labour's attempt at a 1970s Political Programme ended up a failure, and resulted in their being voted out of office on May 3rd, 1979. The party immediately proceeded to dissolve into warring factions, without even waiting for a true Great Endorsement for their rivals. The 1980 Labour Party Conference was a particularly vicious affair. Callaghan resigned as leader soon after and was replaced by Michael Foot, an old trooper of the left who had been one of the authors of *Guilty Men* back in 1940.

Groups like the Trotskyite Militant Tendency began to call for ever more power to be given to party activists. In 1981, the 'Gang of Four' – which included Roy Jenkins – split from Labour and founded the Social Democratic Party.

So that was the 1970s, a strange decade when both parties attempted to launch Political Programmes but neither succeeded, both getting one hand on power but neither receiving the giant 'Yes!' from the voting public that gives a Programme the confidence and time to put its Action Plan into practice, safe in the knowledge of a thumping majority.

Was this due to inept leadership? Maybe a bit, but at a deeper level, there was something unusually febrile about that decade. It really did seem that 'the system' was breaking down. My own belief is that it looked that way because it was true – from late 1973, anyway. The middle years of the decade signalled the end of an era of industrial production and mass consumption based not just on cheap oil but, more lasting, on the belief that the planet could take all the negative externalities we chose to throw at it.

Underlying all the post-war Political Programmes had been a sense that we had a machine chugging nicely along, which generated perpetually increasing wealth. Attlee, Macmillan and Wilson led debates about who should own that machine, how its output should be divided, and how to fine-tune it so it worked best. During the 1970s, a scary thought arose: supposing this machine had a limited life-span and we were reaching the end of that? Supposing, as a popular phrase of the time had it, there were 'no more goodies in the pipeline'?

Frightening, indeed.

At the same time, I love the popular culture of that era, especially the early part. It had a confidence to it: it had big horizons and asked big questions. However, as the decade advanced, it seemed to catch fright. Hollywood suffered a severe case of paranoia, with movies like *The Parallax View* and *The Conversation* (both from 1974) or *Taxi Driver* (1976). It took *Star Wars* (1977) to get the mood simple and upbeat again (but at a cost: wasn't it all a bit formulaic?). British music got angry, via punk, or looked darkly inward in albums like Pink Floyd's *The Wall* (1979). My own sense of the decade is that popular culture had an Icarus-like quality to it, flying free but in the end suffering from damaged wings. (Other people, no doubt, feel different.)

Right at the end of the decade, however, something changed. Not just the arrival of a party with a genuine Political Programme, but, deeper, a new element to the wealth-generating process that didn't deplete irreplaceable resources or spew out pollution. This was Information Technology. For much of the 1970s, computers were vast things, whirring away in their own sealed inner sancta and spewing out reams of lined green paper that only their high priests could understand. But they were evolving fast, becoming ever more compact, powerful, cheaper and user-friendly, and proving useful to organizations of all kinds in all sorts of novel ways. The next decade would see whole new industries come into being.

This did not mean that the economy suddenly stopped pouring rubbish into the environment, but it did mean that it was less profoundly reliant on so doing. 1973 was the year that Britain chucked the most CO_2 into the atmosphere, 660,000 kilotons of the stuff. We are now emitting around 350,000 kilotons, and all major political parties officially want to bring that down to zero. (Sadly for the planet, this trend has only been in the UK and mainland Europe. The USA, Canada and Australia all emit more CO2 than they did in 1973, and the developing countries put out massively more. China, which emitted around 970,000 kilotons in 1973, now produces over 10,000,000 annually.)

As the 1980s unfolded, with the new technological model developing and a new wealth-creating machine getting into gear, politicians would be able to get back to debating ownership, fair shares and optimization, which is what happened before the 1970s and is what has happened since – though we may soon be in for another existential crisis.

The implication of this is that there are technological/economic eras that last much, much longer than any Political Programme. This does not invalidate the Political Programme model. Unless you're Karl Marx, you can have one underlying dominant nexus of technologies and many radically different ways of structuring and organizing society around that nexus, each with its own culture.

Thatcherism, 1979 - 1997

Like Attleean Socialism, Thatcherism had extensive intellectual roots. These date back to 1776, when Adam Smith wrote about a 'hidden hand' guiding the economy. "It is not through the benevolence of the butcher, the brewer or the baker that we expect our dinner, but from their regard to their own interest." Later work by the Austrian and Chicago schools of economics was also required reading for serious Thatcherites. FA von Hayek was particularly favoured. Churchill had cited his *The Road to Serfdom* in 1945, but it been dropped by One Nation Conservatives as too radical. Now it was back. Other key economic texts were Milton Friedman's 1962 *Capitalism and Freedom* and the work of James Buchanan.

These works stressed the efficiency of the free market as a creator and allocator of resources, and the inefficiency of state meddling in it. Buchanan's Public Choice Theory – for which he would win the Nobel Prise in 1986 – modelled the state as parasitic, staffed by 'rent-seeking' individuals maximizing their own utility rather than serving the public. Hayek took this even further, arguing that the state had a natural tendency to become actively tyrannical. For him, market freedom was an essential guarantor of political freedom – the polar opposite of left-wing claims that Capitalism enslaved the individual.

These views constituted a radical break from what had become orthodoxy since 1940: a benign state with the ability and the duty to intervene in markets to engineer socially desirable outcomes. This has led some commentators to argue that the entire time from then (or at least 1945) to 1979 was one ideological period. According to the model presented in this book, that is an oversimplification, though it is undoubtedly true that the Attlee and Thatcher revolutions were particularly deep, as was the New Liberal one of 1906.

As well as powerful Models, Thatcherism had strong Values: hard work, old-school morality. Thatcher had learnt these in her childhood home in Grantham, where her father was a successful businessman but also an active citizen. She carried the *Ten Cannots* of William C H Boetcker (often misattributed to Abraham Lincoln) in her iconic handbag. Compared to Hayek, Friedman or Buchanan, these are pretty homespun, but they have a simple moral force which was an essential part of the new Programme.

As I have said, Thatcherism also had strong First and Second Stories – something not all Political Programmes have. The trade unions, 'big government' and the far left were the Dragons in need of Slaying; entrepreneurs and other 'wealth-creators' the makers of the Bright Future.

These Models, Values and Stories were nurtured and turned into policy options in various think tanks. The free-market Institute for Economic Affairs (IEA) was one, founded in 1955 by Anthony Fisher, who made his fortune from factory farming. After Ted Heath's U-turns, another group of market-minded Tory MPs founded the Selsdon Group, dedicated to carrying on the now-abandoned policies of the 1970 election-winner. However, the main Crucible Group of Thatcherism was the Centre for Policy Studies, founded in 1974 by Keith Joseph, Alfred Sherman and Thatcher herself.

In February 1975, Thatcher was elected the party's leader: the Programme's accession to Significant Influence. The election was the usual complex affair. Heath was knocked out early, and the man she beat in the final ballot was Willie Whitelaw. Heath refused to serve the new Programme in any way, but Whitelaw became Thatcher's Foil, loyal and often a calming influence, until his retirement from politics in December 1987.

Thatcher became Prime Minister in the election of May 1979. Her majority was decent – 43 seats – but she still had an enormous amount of work to do, convincing many of her colleagues (let alone the country) of her radical new Programme. A less firm hand could easily have been shaken off the tiller: this was a First Taste of Power, a trial run, not a great roar of public approval.

The economy plunged into recession, but Thatcher refused to use the traditional Keynesian lever of boosting demand by pumping in money, as in her Model, this would simply reignite inflation. Instead, she stuck to her Core Policy of supply-side reforms, trying to make it easier for businesses to create jobs and wealth.

The recession continued. Party grandees told her she must do a U-turn, but she replied with her 'the lady's not for turning' speech at the 1980 Party Conference at Brighton. In March 1981, 364 leading economists wrote her an open letter via the Times newspaper, criticizing her policies – a classic 'shocked old guard' response of horror: "You can't do that!" She ignored them. Political Programme Leaders sense in their bones that U-turns on Core Policies are fatal.

Many old manufacturing companies went to the wall, but inflation fell, and the economy began to recover, albeit slowly and painfully. However, the party remained unpopular in the polls, despite Labour's almost equally unpopular lurch to the left. A new Alliance Party, formed from a merger of the Liberals and the Social Democrats, began to gain ground.

Would Thatcherism end up another Aspirant Programme that never quite made it?

Some conspiracy theorists say that Thatcher set up the Falklands War, feigning weakness to confuse the macho Argentinian generals. But this doesn't fit the facts. She tried to negotiate via her Foreign Secretary Francis Pym, but was rebuffed. She went to war because she felt she had to defend (very) British citizens against a foreign dictatorship. She took a genuine risk in doing so. The British force was 8,000 miles from home. It was outnumbered. It did not have air superiority. Britain won due to the outstanding qualities of its servicemen and to slices of luck – a number of bombs that hit British ships failed to detonate. So, yes, Britain gained the victory, and the celebration of that victory was the Crowning Glory for the Thatcherite Programme. But, like all true Crowning Glories, it was not set up.

The Great Endorsement duly followed, with a thumping 144 majority in a general election the next year. The Programme, now in its Pomp, got into full gear.

My own personal view is that Thatcher would have seen off her rivals anyway. The Zeitgeist was heading in her direction (more on the culture of the early 80s shortly...)

There had been small privatizations in the first Thatcher government, but a Programme's Pomp is the time when its Action Plan gets fully realized. If you don't carry it out then, you never will. The sale of British Telecom, in 1984, then the biggest state sale of shares ever, raised nearly £4 billion (£15 bn in our fast-depreciating modern money). There were many sceptics, but the sale was a success. It launched a new era of 'popular capitalism', and it also shook up the complacent Post Office –

getting a phone installed in your home or business in the 1970s had been a nightmare. Other privatizations included British Gas (with its adverts telling 'Sid' about it), British Airways, a large part of BP and, later, the nation's ten water utilities. The model was copied around the world, earning British consultancy firms huge fees for advising other governments on the process.

Entrepreneurship was encouraged. Wilsonian planners hadn't understood enterprise (which doesn't fit plans). Old-school Tories, by and large, preferred dealing with large, established businesses: entrepreneurs were a bit flash for them. The new Programme introduced entrepreneur-friendly policies such as the Small Firms Loan Guarantee and the Enterprise Allowance Schemes. Top rates of tax were slashed. Maybe an even bigger boost came from the change of tone. Entrepreneurs were suddenly feted. Sir Richard Branson, one of the most successful of them, said of Thatcher, "She really did set the groundwork for entrepreneurialism in Britain."

Pomp is also time for a Programme's Big Battles, in this case with the trade unions. There were two such conflicts: the year-long miners' strike of 1984/5 and the even longer print-workers' strike of 1986/7. The former was the most dramatic, while the latter was arguably more emblematic of changing times, with Fleet Street printers resisting the introduction of new technology. Both involved violence at scary levels. Neither could have been won without a Great Endorsement, both in parliament and in the public mood.

Another Big Battle was with the Soviet Empire. The fall of the Berlin Wall in 1989 was arguably the Programme's ultimate Big Win, six years into its Pomp. This was, of course, an allied effort, not just a British one. But Thatcher sympathized more and worked more closely with US

President Ronald Reagan than did any other European leader. When deployed in 1983, more US cruise missiles were put in Britain than in any other European country. She then led the way in dealing with Mikhail Gorbachev, inviting him to Chequers in 1984, even before he met Reagan.

One can argue that, once the old era of oil-based heavy industry had been replaced by the agile new one of IT, the oil-rich, heavy-industry-loving Soviet Union was doomed. But dying empires can be vicious. The end of the Cold War was a relatively gentle affair. That almost bloodless victory was an outstanding achievement, in which Mrs Thatcher played a key role. Sadly, the standard narcissistic, infantile rage of collapsing empires was not soothed in Russia in 1989 after all, but simply repressed. It is acting itself out now, instead.

The Programme's economic liberalism was not matched in the social sphere. The apartheid regime in South Africa was tolerated, and even welcomed as a strategic ally. Homosexuality wasn't recriminalized, but a bizarre section in the 1988 Local Government Act insisted that Local Authorities should not 'intentionally promote' it. 'Promoting' was interpreted as any attempt to educate young people about the reality of different sexual orientations. Gay people who grew up in that era speak of 'Section 28' with intense bitterness: it was seen as a charter for homophobia and bullying.

The Archetype of the Thatcher years was the 'Yuppie'. Many young people no longer wanted to find their own way, as they had done in the late sixties and the seventies, but to do whatever was required in order to make money. Money, regarded as a bit grubby in the 1970s, suddenly conferred status. Yuppies could be of either gender; women reached out for power and took it, 'power dressing' to make the point.

Waves of brassy blockbuster movies flowed across the Atlantic. Popular music became smart and snappy, with synths and drum machines elbowing out guitars and wild, long-haired drummers (the first commercially available drum machine, the Linn LM-1, came out in 1980, the same year that Led Zeppelin's John Bonham died). Watch Duran Duran going sailing in 1982 on the video for *Rio*. Those young men on their yacht – are those pastel suits waterproof? – are riding the waves off the coast of some tropical paradise, but also the wave of a new era and its Zeitgeist.

There was also a strong Counterblast. In popular culture, songs like The Specials' 1981 *Ghost Town* protested the economic damage caused by the refusal to reflate. In the world of 'higher' culture, Mrs Thatcher had a small group of supporters, such as former Angry Young Man Kingsley Amis, novelist Anthony Powell and poet Philip Larkin, but the majority opinion was one of horror. The rising novelists of the era, such as Salman Rushdie, Julian Barnes or Amis' son Martin, despised her. Amis's *Money* is a particularly vicious satire on the spiritually destructive artifice and excess of the era.

Critics of high culture said that just showed how stuck-up its exponents were. One certainly has to look hard to see any literary novel or serious film from the era that treats the adventure of entrepreneurship with the sensitivity that Peter Smith and Dilip Hiro's *A Private Enterprise* did back in 1974. *My Beautiful Laundrette*, from 1985, comes closest. The only established art where the Programme had real influence was architecture, where the functional 60s and 70s modernism associated with Wilsonian planning came under attack, and a new, flamboyant post-modern style blossomed. If you live in London, go to Richmond, stroll along the Thames and enjoy Quinlan Terry's Riverside development. (If you take a detour to Kew, you can bask in the spirit of an earlier entrepreneurial era, the 1840s, courtesy of the great Palm House built in that decade.)

At the 1989 Party Conference, delegates chanted "Ten More Years!" But Political Programmes don't last that long.

Thatcherism's First Big Failure was the Community Charge, better known as the poll tax. This was the culmination of a long-running battle between the Programme and its opponents in high-spending local councils. Councils were partially funded by 'rates' levied on homeowners and businesses. The Conservatives had long considered this unfair, but couldn't agree how to replace them. One idea, suggested early on in the Programme's life, was a poll tax, levied equally on every adult. This was rejected as even more unfair: the very poor would be supposed to stump up exactly the same as the very rich. (There had been no such taxes in England since the seventeenth century, and an earlier one, in 1381, had led to armed revolution.) However, the battle between the Programme and far-left councils intensified over the decade, and finally the Conservatives decided to introduce a poll tax after all. This was done with some misgivings, but the PM was adamant. At one point, she went as far as to declare that the new tax was the 'flagship' of her fleet.

The tax was introduced in Scotland in 1989 (the Scottish Conservatives had been particularly strong advocates of the tax). The reaction to it was immediate and negative, with many people refusing to pay.

Time to halt the experiment? No, the tax was rolled out in England and Wales the next year. It was a disaster. March 1990 saw a large protest rally in Central London, that turned into a riot. More significantly, the 'silent majority' was unimpressed. One opinion poll said that 75% of the population were against the tax – and polls generally began giving Labour huge leads.

146

Now time to stop? The fleet sailed on, heading straight for the rocks.

At this point, readers might object that my model says that Political Programmes shouldn't make U-turns, as Heath did. Am I now saying Thatcher should have made one?

Yes. There is a crucial difference between the two situations. For all Thatcher's talk of 'flagships', the poll tax was not part of the Programme's Big Idea, which was about freeing up enterprise. The tax was not a Core Policy presented to, and massively endorsed by, the electorate. It was a piece of Normal Politics, added to a to-do list late in the career of that Programme. Yes, it was in the 1987 manifesto, but right near the end – a very odd place for a 'flagship' policy. As a piece of Normal Politics, the tax could easily have been ditched. Doing so would not have damaged the essential core of Thatcherism, just the Leader's ego.

The Worldview, Action Plan and Big Idea of full-on Political Programmes have a Darwinian robustness. They are forged in heated debate, then have to battle for wider acceptance: first within the party, then among the electorate, who will be sceptical to start with but are finally won over. 'Normal' policy ideas, at best thought up to respond to newly emerging problems, do not have the same steely evolutionary history. They may turn out to be genuinely good – but they may not, and need to be treated with healthy, Popperian scepticism. The poll tax was a piece of Normal Politics that did not work well. Treated like a Core Policy and forced through against both the popular will and common sense, it did great damage to the Programme.

It didn't totally crash it, however. The Conservatives managed to recover in the opinion polls, but somehow they felt weak and out of touch from then on. Six months later, the Leader was ousted in a spat over Europe

147

– an issue which became the Big Split for the Programme.

A classic Replacement Leader, John Major, was chosen. His pleasant character probably won him a close election in 1992 (as Clement Attlee showed, British electors can warm to decent, quiet people). However, his 21-seat win in April 1992 was no Great Endorsement.

His success did not last long. In September of that year, the Programme received its Body-blow, when the UK crashed out of the European Exchange Rate Mechanism, a group of European currencies that tried to keep their values similar to one another. In 1990, Major, then chancellor, had joined it, hoping it would keep inflation down. But he had entered at an unsustainable level (an unfortunate echo of Churchill's entry to the gold standard in the Baldwin years). In mid-September 1992, speculators began shorting the currency. The government spent billions of pounds trying to support it. Interest rates were put up to 1970s levels, which terrified the life out of mortgaged homeowners. The selling went on. At 7.00 on the evening of Wednesday, September 16th, chancellor Norman Lamont pulled the plug and exited the Mechanism.

A core part of Thatcherism's appeal had lain in the sense that the Conservatives 'got' the economy and were good at managing it, unlike 'head in the clouds' Socialists. After 'Black Wednesday', that no longer rang true. Ironically, the economy did well in the later part of the Major years, but perception is a key aspect of politics. From October 1992 till the 1997 election, not a single poll shows a Tory lead. Instead they almost all show double-digit leads for Labour. Two polls at the end of 1994 gave the 'reds' a lead of over 40%.

The Programme's Big Split grew ever wider. Tory Eurosceptics carried on a running battle with the administration as it tried to ratify the EU's

Maastricht Treaty in parliament. After the ratification finally succeeded, in July 1993, a tape was left running after an interview: Major was heard referring to three Eurosceptic ministers as 'bastards'.

A Slow Strangler soon prowled into view, as well: 'sleaze', a set of scandals about senior Tory figures' private lives and financial dealings. At the Split-riven 1993 Party Conference, Major made a speech about getting 'back to basics'. He was talking about old-fashioned decency and kindness in public life – an appeal that came naturally to him. But many in his party, including its Director of Communications, took it as a rallying cry to 'roll back the permissive society' and return to old-fashioned values: no sex before marriage, fidelity after it and a disapproval of homosexuality. Major, now desperate to maximize party unity, didn't disabuse these people of this misunderstanding: the rollers-back of permissiveness were often also strong Eurosceptics, and this was some way of appearing to share ground with them.

This was another piece of broken-Programme Normal Politics, an attempt to invent policy on the hoof, partially in the hope that voters might like it, but more to shore up internal party arguments. PR disasters followed almost at once. Two weeks later, it was revealed that a junior Tory minister, recently split from his wife, had three lovers, none of whom knew of the others' existence, and had had two other lovers while still married. This earned him some admiration for his energy but none for his authenticity in spouting an anti-permissive message. A second MP who had talked of 'reducing the number of single parents' turned out to have an illegitimate child himself. Another aspect of 'basics' was financial probity. A series of scandals – 'arms for Iraq', 'cash for questions' – quickly put paid to the administration's reputation for this.

Arguably, a second Slow Strangler was Northern Ireland, where progress towards peace seemed painfully slow. Major, as always, tried his best, but there was too much historic distrust on the Republican side. Since 1912, the Conservatives had been technically called the 'Conservative and Unionist Party', and the party had been associated with Unionism well before that – it had been a Core Policy of Lord Salisbury's Political Programme back in 1895.

Despite these, in the early 1990s there was no compelling alternative to the 'Thatcherism Lite' model on offer, so British politics went into a state of Drift.

The spirit of the age was much less timorous: it wanted change. Artists duly obliged. Richard Curtis' movie *Four Weddings and a Funeral* (with its opening salvo of f-words that horrified the Thatcher generation) and Louis de Bernières' novel *Captain Corelli's Mandolin* both date from 1994. Unlike the buttoned-down, materialistic world of Thatcherism, these were unashamedly romantic and artistic. Their world is one where love, not cash, triumphs. But they were also different to the self-consciously literary Counterblast prizewinners of the Thatcher era. *Corelli* was both literary and delightfully approachable – a symbol of a new, mass 'small l' liberalism. It was a favourite with Book Clubs, a key cultural phenomenon of the time, which kicked off in America with Oprah Winfrey's club in 1996 but soon flourished over here.

Similarly, the great Britpop acts, Blur, Oasis and Pulp, battled it out in the days of the Major administration but were heralds of a world to come. The same can be said for the club, Ministry of Sound, and the feisty Spice Girls, who had stormed the charts in 1996.

All that was needed was a new Political Programme to catch this new cultural wave...

Thatcherism

Leader: Margaret Thatcher

Foil: Willie Whitelaw

Replacement Leader: John Major

Core Policies: Privatization, low taxes, monetarist macroeconomics, face down trade unions, encourage entrepreneurship

Crucible Group: Centre for Policy Studies

Sacred Texts: Smith, Hayek, Friedman, the 'Ten Cannots'

Archetypes: Yuppie, small business owner

Villains: USSR, trade unions, 'scroungers', inflation, the state

Bright Future: economic freedom and growth

Gaining Significant Influence: Thatcher becomes Party Leader, 1975

First Taste of Power: Election victory of 1979

Crowning Glory: Victory in the Falklands War

Great Endorsement: 144-seat victory in 1983

Cultural Endorsements: *Rio* video, 1982. Quinlan Terry, *Richmond Riverside*

Counterblasts: *Ghost Town*, The Specials. *Money*, Martin Amis

Big Wins: Conquest of inflation, privatization, defeat of unions, End of Cold War

Big Battles: With NUM and print unions

First Big Failure: Poll tax

Body-blow: Black Wednesday, 16th September 1992

Big Split: Europhiles vs. Eurosceptics

Slow Stranglers: 'Back to basics'/sleaze, Northern Ireland

Dethronement/Waterloo: Labour Landslide of 1997

New Labour, 1997 - 2010

Most Political Programmes gain power in two steps. First there is a provisional First Taste. The nation is excited, but also still asking: 'Do we *really* want this?' If the Programme and its people have got what it takes, the answer is 'Yes', and they go on to get a Landslide. New Labour's trajectory was different. A new mood grew during the mid-1990s, and the Programme grew with it, but both had to wait till the electoral cycle played itself out. By May 1997, the nation was waiting with open arms for the new Programme.

I'm not sure there was a Sacred Text for it. Maybe parts of Crosland's *Future of Socialism* qualify, where he talked of the need for a brighter Britain. Or Jenkins' *The Labour Case*. Sociologist Anthony Giddens, who wrote a number of books at the start of the 1990s about a 'Third Way' between socialism and capitalism, influenced many Programme supporters. However, the Programme Leader, Tony Blair, makes no reference to any of these works in his autobiography.

More influential on Blair was European civilization's original Sacred Text, the Bible. One has to go back to Stanley Baldwin to find a Programme Leader for whom Christianity mattered as much. Blair's faith was very different to that of the pipe-smoking Tory gentleman. Strongly influenced by philosopher John Macmurray and Peter Thomson, a rebellious Australian mature student he met at Oxford, it was egalitarian and anti-establishment.

Or maybe the Sacred Texts weren't texts at all but 60s and 70s rock, with its insistence on emotional intensity and personal authenticity. Blair tried his hand as a music promoter as a young man, then sang in a student band. There is a great divide between people who came of age in the fifties/early-1960s and those who did so in the late-1960s/seventies. Blair was the first UK Programme Leader to be on the modern, rock'n'roll side of that divide.

There was no Crucible Group, either. The nearest thing was a Crucible duet. As a newly-elected MP in 1983, Blair shared an office with another new arrival, Gordon Brown, and they spent many hours discussing all aspects of policy. Both were seen as 'men with a future' in the party. Initially, Brown, who was slightly older and had deeper roots in the Labour movement, was looked on as the potential leader. But Blair edged past him. After the untimely death of party leader John Smith in May 1994, Blair ran for leadership. He reputedly did a deal with Brown over dinner at a restaurant in New Labour's spiritual home, Islington, that if he (Brown) did not stand against him, he (Blair) would give Brown considerable power and would hand over the PM's job to him after two terms in office.

Blair then won the leadership race, a convoluted process, at the end of that year. The Programme had acquired Significant Influence.

Blair consolidated his power in the party. Clause IV, its 77-year-old commitment to massive nationalization, was abolished in 1995. He gathered an Action Group around him: himself, Brown, Alistair Campbell, Peter Mandelson, PR expert Anji Hunter and former diplomat Jonathan Powell. In pursuit of electoral victory, he even wooed right-wing media mogul Rupert Murdoch.

In 1997, New Labour leapfrogged any gentle First Taste of Power and jumped straight to a Great Endorsement – the greatest in the post-war era – seizing total, confident control in a Landslide electoral win. The 179-seat majority was the biggest for a political party since Baldwin's in 1924, bigger than anything achieved by Attlee or Thatcher.

Blair's Programme has been accused of being light on policy, but this is unfair. Maybe it listened to focus groups too much, but that was mainly about tweaking Normal Politics. It had a clear Worldview and Action Plan and stuck to it for a long time. It had much more respect for market mechanisms than previous Labour Programmes, which had seen them as wild, amoral things which needed taming by planners. New Labour sought a middle way, admiring markets' (and especially entrepreneurs') capacity to generate wealth but also understanding that markets are not perfectly efficient or always morally good. Serious money would be spent on public goods such as health and education. A new marriage of private and public was planned.

This was novel, but the heart of the Programme's vision was cultural and social. Unlike Thatcherism, which had introduced the anti-gay Section 28 legislation and lectured us about 'back to basics', New Labour championed diversity and inclusiveness. There were twice as many women in the new parliament than in the previous one – 101 out of the 120 being on the Labour benches. Homophobia and racism were taboo (though parliament still had few black, Asian or minority-ethnic MPs). The Programme set a radically fresh tone: tolerant, young, metropolitan, intelligent, able, international, open, emotionally literate.

There was a culture waiting with open arms to celebrate this vision. It had already spoken, though *Four Weddings*, *Captain Corelli*, Britpop, the Spice Girls and Ministry of Sound. The year of the Programme's Great Endorsement, saw the radical *Sensation* exhibition by Young British

Artists at London's Royal Academy of Arts. More significant for the general public, that year also saw the publication of the first volume of the Harry Potter series. JK Rowling's novels had strong messages of anti-racism and individual empowerment, but cloaked them in the kind of witty fantasy that hard-headed Thatcherites despised. The books (and, later, the movies) became for the new Programme what The Beatles had been for Harold Wilson in 1964: a global advertisement, infinitely more powerful than any political speeches or GDP figures, that new-look Britain was onto something. The media talked of 'Cool Britannia'.

There was very little Counterblast.

Arguably, the new Programme had a Crowning Glory a couple of nights after its Landslide, when the UK's Katrina and the Waves stormed to an equally large victory in the Eurovision Song Contest. Europe was watching the new government and approved. The winning song, *Love, Shine a Light,* had originally been written as an anthem for the Samaritans, an organization dedicated to helping people with suicidal thoughts by listening to them down a phone line – sentiments in line with the new Programme's Worldview and unlike the old Programme's world of the 'stiff upper lip'.

On home ground, the Programme's uninvited triumph came with the death of Princess Diana. Four months after Blair's victory, the nation awoke to the news. Early that morning, a few people came to lay flowers outside Kensington Palace. That trickle of mourners soon turned into to a flood. The nation was expressing grief in what seemed a totally new way (though anyone who had been at the Cenotaph in 1919 would have understood). There was a sense that the people of the UK had been to a therapy session, asked to look at their own buried unhappinesses, and had suddenly burst into tears.

Blair intuitively understood and respected this. Asked to respond to the death, he gave a simple but heartfelt speech. (One can never tell with professional politicians, but when he said he was 'utterly devasted', the look on his face seemed to match the words. Watch the video.) By contrast, the Conservative Party looked wooden and embarrassed. One felt that it wanted to slap Britain round the face and tell the nation to bloody well snap out of it. The party also had a young leader, William Hague, but he as was bemused by the public reaction as his older colleagues. One such colleague, a former member of John Major's cabinet, told journalist Matthew D'Ancona: "I walked through the crowds in St James's, and realised this was no longer a country I truly understand." Such are changes of eras and their Zeitgeist.

It seems odd to talk of this as a Glory, but, as with the great mass mournings of 1919 and 1920 – if D'Ancona's former minister had read more history, he might have been less baffled – it was an unscripted mass demonstration of emotion exactly in tune with the tone of the newly endorsed Political Programme, which is what a Crowning Glory is.

The new government soon secured some Big Wins. In 1998, a national minimum wage was introduced. As at the start of Thatcherism, a number of economists said this policy wouldn't work. This was ignored, and the policy has been retained ever since.

The same year saw the Good Friday Agreement in Northern Ireland. New governmental institutions were set up in the province: the Northern Ireland Assembly and Executive, with the latter based on 'power-sharing' between Unionists and Irish Nationalists (as opposed to a system where a majority ruled the roost). Bodies were created to facilitate dialogue between Eire, the Six Counties and Britain. Most important of all, the major paramilitary organizations agreed to renounce violence.

After three decades of horrific killings, this was a massive achievement.

Other Big Wins include the setting up of the Sure Start programme for nurseries, the creation of a separate government Department for International Development and a genuine redistribution of wealth via changes to the tax and benefits system. According to some estimates, around 2 million people were lifted out of poverty by New Labour.

History, of course, was waiting, Voldemort-like, to trip up the new Programme. New Labour had a long, vigorous Pomp, but its First Big Failure duly arrived in 2003, when the Leader went to war in Iraq. He did so with hardly any support with our European allies and against the wishes of a million people who marched through London on February 15th of that year to protest.

There was a quick, impressive military victory, followed by helpless, ever-deepening entanglement in Iraqi politics. There had been inadequate planning as to what would happen after we won. Our intended liberation of that complex, divided country soon turned into occupation, and this became a recruiting-call for terrorists, especially after the interrogation procedures at Abu Ghraib prison became public knowledge. This would have a horrific pay-off with the 2005 London attacks.

After the war, no Weapons of Mass Destruction (WMD) were found in Iraq. Suspicion began to grow that a dossier produced by the government in September 2002, purportedly full of objective information about the country's possession of WMD, had been 'sexed up' to promote the war. A whistleblower to this effect, Dr David Kelly, was found dead in July 2003 – most likely a case of suicide, but suicide brought on by political pressure placed on him.

Blair's personal credibility was seriously damaged. His reputation for competence suffered from the disastrous occupation. His reputation for honesty – a major part of his appeal in 1997, contrasting with 'Tory sleaze' – suffered from the suspicions about the dossier, even though he was later officially cleared of any wrongdoing. New Labour had always relied heavily on 'spin', on the framing and selection of facts to prove a case. Many people thought the dossier had crossed the fuzzy boundary between spin and outright lying.

However, the Programme was not destroyed by Iraq. The polls for 2003 did see the end of double-figure support, but there was no love-fest for the Conservatives. Neutral for a year or so, the figures turn consistently red again in mid-2004. In its third election, in 2005, the Programme's majority was cut by more than half, but it was still a tidy 66 seats. Iraq was a First Big Failure, not a Body-blow.

That was the financial crisis of 2007/8. Old Labour had seen the City as a posh casino, the home of privileged speculators with more loyalty to Zurich gnomes than to the nation. To New Labour, it was an essential part of the modern economy, providing 'financial services'. It made huge amounts of money that was spent in booming London and that could be taxed to support worthwhile projects like the NHS, Sure Start or Tax Credits. In the New Labour worldview, the markets in which the City operated were not casino tables but efficient Hayekian mechanisms for allocating capital. Maybe in the old days there had been spectacular crashes, but New Labour knew better. The dotcom boom and bust around the turn of the millennium had been dramatic but the economy had quickly recovered. New Labour carried forward the Thatcherite approach to the City, which was to keep it deregulated.

The crisis broke on September 14th, 2007, when Northern Rock, a once aptly-named old-style building society that had embraced the new world of financial deregulation and turned itself into a rather racy bank offering 125% mortgages, applied to the Bank of England for support – in other words, went bust.

Things grew worse in March 2008, when Bear Stearns, the most risk-loving of Wall Street's big investment banks, went under. In September of that year, Lehmann Brothers, an institution with a theoretically much more solid reputation, filed for bankruptcy. Royal Bank of Scotland, which had embarked on a decade-long acquisition spree based on debt, looked set to follow it. Suddenly the entire financial system – the global one, not just Britain's – looked about to come crashing down in a rerun, not of the 2000 dotcom shake-out but of the catastrophe of the 1930s.

Blair had handed over power to his former lieutenant Gordon Brown in June 2007. Like Ted Heath, the newcomer was unlucky with his timing. However, Brown handled the crisis superbly. Arguably he did more to save the global financial system than anyone else. Huge amounts of money were thrown, decisively and quickly, at debt-ridden banks to prevent runs on them. The system pulled through. A grateful nation responded by…

…Saying it would vote Conservative at the next election. From September 2007, the polls almost all show Tory support, and from mid-2008, that support is in double figures. The Body-blow that was the 2008 crisis destroyed core beliefs in the Programme's Worldview, that markets could be relied upon and that the City was a risk-free tax cow.

The nation was left with a weak economy. There was a level of debt not seen since the 1960s, when we were still paying off the cost of World War Two. There was little money for business to invest in creating greater productivity (productivity, which is what a successful economy is based on, had been quietly rising in since 1990, but virtually flattened out after 2008). New thinking was required, but in the Worldview of the Blairite Political Programme, there was only one way to reduce the debt: cut government expenditure and then plod painfully back to a more sustainable level. So that was what was done. This was a bitter U-turn for the once free-spending New Labour. 'Austerity' placed much of the burden of the debt recovery on the very people New Labour had set out to help, the poor. It quickly became a Slow Strangler for the Programme.

A second Strangler was the Programme's tone. A sense developed that its smart metropolitan leaders, compassionate in some ways, looked down on older, provincial types, secretly considering them racist, sexist, homophobic, vulgarly nationalistic and generally obsolete. This perceived dismissiveness was summed up in an incident during the 2010 election campaign, when Gillian Duffy, a 65-year-old retired council worker who had lived in Rochdale (and voted Labour) all her life, questioned Gordon Brown on a number of issues, including immigration from Eastern Europe. After their brief conversation, a microphone picked up Brown complaining that she should not have been let near him, adding, "She was just a sort of bigoted woman."

Such condescension had been foreseen in Michael Young's *The Rise of the Meritocracy* back in 1958. 'Meritocracy' (a word he invented) is often thought of as desirable, better than old fashioned class advantage, but the book was actually a warning. Young's meritocrats were ruthless. The old class overlords, like most Fifties Conservatives, had possessed a sense of *noblesse oblige*. Meritocrats, Young reckoned, would have no such sense. They believed they had earned their status and felt free to despise the less successful.

The same warning has recently been reissued by American philosopher Michael J Sandel in *The Tyranny of Merit*.

Labour lost the 2010 election, and a hung parliament resulted. Gordon Brown resigned, and in the subsequent leadership contest between the Miliband brothers, the 'Blairite' David was defeated by the more left-of-centre Ed. End of Programme…

…In a way. However, it wasn't replaced by anything radically different. A period of Drift followed. It wouldn't be till the middle of the decade that a fully new Political Programme, with truly different policies and, most important of all, culture, would arise.

New Labour

Leader: Tony Blair

Foil: Gordon Brown

Sacred Texts: (?) The work of Anthony Giddens, rock'n'roll

Core Policies: Social liberalism, inclusivity, 'Market Socialism'

Carried Forward: Respect for enterprise, a deregulated City

Crucible Group: Blair and Brown

Action Group: Them plus Mandelson, Campbell, Hunter, Powell

Archetypes: 'New man', post-feminist woman

Bright Future: Economic growth in a society free of prejudice

Gaining Significant Influence: Blair becomes party Leader

First Taste of Power: Election victory of 1997

Great Endorsement: The same (!)

Crowning Glory: Public mourning for Diana, Princess of Wales

Cultural Endorsements: *Four Weddings and a Funeral*, *Captain Corelli's Mandolin*, *Sensation* exhibition, *Love Shine a Light*, Harry Potter, 'Cool Britannia'

Big Wins: Minimum wage, Good Friday Agreement, Increased NHS spending, Tax credits

First Big Failure: Iraq War (2003)

Body-blow: 2007/8 crisis and subsequent U-turn on spending

Slow Stranglers: Austerity, disconnect with provincial Labour voters

Dethronement: 2010 election

Waterloo: 2016 referendum

The Coalition Years, 2010 - 2015

A few dramatic days followed the 2010 election result, at the end of which a Coalition was agreed between the Conservatives (who had received most votes and most seats) and the Liberal Democrats.

Together, the two parties had a majority of 72. A Great Endorsement? I find it hard to argue that this was a proper Political Programme. The electorate hadn't fully endorsed either of the parties – the 'endorsement' came simply from adding together two groups of people who had voted for different leaders and policies.

The Coalition carried forward much of the spirit of New Labour: wisely, perhaps, as that still seemed to be the dominant national mood, despite the problems with debt and austerity. Both the Conservatives' David Cameron and his Lib Dem colleague Nick Clegg were chips off the Blair block: young, London-based, cultured, intelligent, internationally-minded and socially liberal. Cameron saw himself as a modernizer of his Party, just as Blair had modernized his. Under his watch, the number of female Conservative MPs doubled, just as the number of female Labour MPs had doubled under Blair. He 'got' popular culture. Unlike Blair he never fronted a band – it's an amusing thought what a Cameron-fronted band might have been like. But unlike most Thatcher-era Tories, he liked popular music, citing Mancunian miserabilists The Smiths as his favourite band was when he was a teenager.

The Coalition Conservatives' ideas were based around Cameron's notion of the 'Big Society'. This marked a major shift from Thatcherism, whose leader had notably said there was 'no such thing' as society. It was also a shift from the centralizing New Labour: Cameron said that the days of big government were over. Decision-making would be pushed away from Westminster and closer to citizens. Rather than boss us around, the government would 'nudge' us into more helpful behaviours, such as healthy eating.

A Sacred Text for the new Conservatism was Philip Blond's *Red Tory*, which criticized both overzealous market devotees and traditional bossy Socialists for squeezing communities and civic organizations. Blond argued that this pincer movement by large, impersonal forces had taken away individual responsibility and a sense of citizenship, and a new Conservative administration should work at putting these back at the heart of national life. (Clement Attlee had sought to reinstate similar values, though he had a different solution.)

The Liberal Democrats had their own differently coloured Sacred Text, *The Orange Book (Reclaiming Liberalism)*. This recast liberalism from a centre-left movement (the way it had been since the last time it had truly led a full-on Political Programme, from 1906 to 1916) to one much more favourable to the free market. At the same time, they retained their commitment to individual liberty. Gladstone would have approved. They now had a First Taste of Power – their first, since 1922. Next step, a Great Endorsement?

Coalition policies included the beefing up of the apprenticeship system, the introduction of a 'pupil premium' to help schools in poorer areas, the legalization of same-sex marriage and a commitment to spend 0.7% of GNP on overseas aid. All of these were small-l liberal, effectively in the New Labour tradition. Less liberal were the new 'Hostile Environment' policy of the Home Office to put off immigrants, and the threefold rise in student fees. The latter was diametrically contrary to the

Liberals' election promises to abolish them. This U-turn was a self-inflicted Body-blow for the Coalition's junior party, and would prove fatal to it at the next election. It is still struggling to recover.

However, the Programme generated no fresh policies for the biggest problem faced by the country at the time, which was the debt burden. Instead, they just ploughed on with austerity. Yes, Political Programmes carry forward ideas from their predecessors, but it is very dangerous to carry forward ideas that have been Slow Stranglers for their predecessors. But that is what the Coalition did, continuing to cut spending on the provision of public goods so that the poor suffered most. Rather than attack the old Strangler with a brave new policy, the Coalition treated it like an unbreakable family curse. As a result of this, the Big Society started to feel more and more like a Slogan – the Coalition's Society was clearly not Big enough to tackle this problem.

Maybe because people sensed this, there was very little spontaneous Cultural Endorsement for the new administration. The determination of Cameron and Clegg to work together was generally liked, but there was no sense of a blast of radical fresh air. Coalition had a pleasant vibe, but wasn't invigorating, in the way that full-on, new Political Programmes are.

In the world of popular books, the big thing was EL James' *Fifty Shades of Grey*, published in 2012. At the same time, the music charts were dominated by acts such as Little Mix and One Direction, created by Simon Cowell though his TV talent show, *The X Factor*. All these works can be criticized as triumphs of style over substance, though this is a little unfair. *Fifty Shades* broke new grounds in public taste with its descriptions of BDSM lovemaking. The singers in these bands had genuine talent, though would not have become superstars without the Cowell machine behind them. A similar criticism can, perhaps, be levelled at the Coalition, and especially Cameron. For Simon Cowell, read his political advisers, Steve Hilton and Lynton Crosby.

Culturally, the most significant mood of the era was probably of Counterblast. Ken Loach's movie, *I, Daniel Blake*, which described the battles of a well-meaning working-class man against the bureaucracy of the benefit system, was written during the Coalition era, though it actually appeared on our screens in 2016.

The administration did have a Crowning Glory, the 2012 London Olympics – though these had been a New Labour idea. The Games are, perhaps, better seen as a celebration of the small-l liberal spirit that straddled both New Labour and the Coalition. Danny Boyle and Frank Cottrell Boyce's opening ceremony was a magnificent love letter to the (then) modern nation. It was quirky, diverse, passionate, moving and infused with humour. The multi-ethnic Team GB performed brilliantly, coming third in the table with 29 gold medals (at Atlanta in 1996, we had won one gold, putting us 36th in the table). As the fireworks lit up the East London sky at the closing ceremony – an event watched by a TV audience of 26 million, a figure second only to Princess Diana's funeral – one could be forgiven for thinking that austerity was just a passing phase and that Britain had found its tone for the new century: youthful, diverse, creative, curious, outward-looking, broad-minded and ambitious, both intellectually and emotionally.

Nothing is forever, in the Zeitgeist or in politics. The Olympics were more a swansong of small-l liberalism than a coronation. Other voices were soon demanding to be heard.

The Coalition Years

Leaders: David Cameron (Conservative), Nick Clegg (Lib Dem)

Carried forward: Youthful attitude, sophistication, social liberalism

Core Policies: Devolve power from state to citizen

Sacred Text: (for Conservatives) *Red Tory*, (for Lib Dems) *The Orange Book*

First Taste of Power: 2010 election victory

Cultural Endorsement: *Fifty Shades of Grey*, The X Factor

Counterblast: Ken Loach, *I, Daniel Blake*

Crowning Glory: (?) 2012 Olympics

Slow Strangler: Austerity

Body-blow: (for Lib Dems) Tripling of student fees

Dethronement: 2015 election

Waterloo: 2016 Brexit referendum

Populist 'Brexit' Nationalism, 2016 - present

I say that politicians grab rising new Zeitgeists and ride them to glory – but some politicians have a long wait before they can do that. The success of the Populist 'Brexit' Nationalism Programme is a lesson in patience. Keep blowing your trumpet, even if large sections of the political establishment are laughing at you, and maybe, just maybe, you will suddenly find an orchestra filling in behind you.

Arguably the first full-on Eurosceptic Crucible Group was the Bruges Group, named for a speech given by Mrs Thatcher in the Belgian city in 1988, that would become a Sacred Text for the Brexit Programme. The group was not founded by political insiders but by an Oxford student, Patrick Robertson, but it soon attracted big names such as former president of the IEA, Ralph Harris. In 1990 Thatcher became its honorary president. Within the Conservative Party, opposition to the EU (as it was called after 1992) coalesced into the European Research Group, founded in 1993 by MP Michael Spicer. An early Eurosceptic Action Group was founded by academic Alan Sked in 1991. His Anti-Federalist League put up candidates in the 1992 election…

…and hardly got any votes. The party was renamed UKIP in 1993. For a while, it was eclipsed by a newer anti-EU party, the Referendum Party, bankrolled by magnate Sir James Goldsmith. This, too, failed at the polls (in 1997). It then disappeared, leaving UKIP to pick up the flickering Eurosceptic torch again. For a long while after that, Brexiter Crucible Groups churned out papers which were eagerly read by other Eurosceptics, while UKIP stood in elections and just managed to outperform the Monster Raving Loony Party.

However, things changed in 2006, when the charismatic Nigel Farage became party Leader. Populism got further boosts in 2007/8 and in 2009 from the crisis and the MPs' expenses scandals. However the real explosion of UKIP support came in 2012/3. Its regular poll ratings of around 5% before March 2012 tripled to 15% or more in a year. In October 2014, it won its first by-election, ex-Tory Douglas Carswell getting a stunning 59.7% of the votes. This was the second biggest election swing in UK political history. Something was stirring.

What exactly? Farage had been working hard on widening the party's appeal from specific anti-Europeanism to broader populist themes of anti-elitism and anti-immigration. The latter, sadly, seems to have been a powerful force: the early 2010s saw rising concern at immigration into the EU from Africa and the Middle East. There was also a rising populist tone around Europe and the USA: this wasn't just a UK phenomenon. But none of those factors totally explains the rise. Set up by long-term pressures, enthusiasm for an Aspirant Programme can smoulder for a long while, then suddenly burst into flame for no obvious reason. Such is the way of Zeitgeists. Memo to anyone seeking to create a Political Programme: keep spreading your message with passion and confidence. Suddenly, for reasons you can't quite understand, people will – or at least, may – start turning round and saying, "Yes! Of course!"

This sudden rise in UKIP support panicked the Conservative leadership. In January 2013, the new Aspirant Brexit Programme gained Significant Influence when David Cameron gave a speech promising a referendum on EU membership. He could not, of course, deliver one, as he was in coalition with the Euro-friendly Liberal Democrats (who by then must have been thinking that they should have teamed up with Labour back in 2010). But the promise was made, so if the Tories won the next election, due in 2015...

They did, with a small (12 seats) but clear majority. But the country's swing to the right was bigger, with UKIP getting 12.6% of the votes (over half as much again as the broken Lib Dems). UKIP's rise did not result in parliamentary seats, but the message was unambiguous. The referendum was set for 23 June 2016.

The Brexiters' Action Groups were energetic, focused and savvy. They used the latest data-capture and analysis technology to target individuals online with extraordinary precision, and succeeded in galvanizing new votes – not the young, but older people who had given up hope in the system ever delivering anything for them. Clutches of newly-motivated voters are often a key part of a new Programme's success.

The nation voted to leave, albeit narrowly. This was the First Taste of Power for the new Programme. From 23 June on, the Brexiters ('Brexiteers' in the Programme's Stories, an extra *e* added to make their Heroes sound like buccaneers) were the most powerful force in the land.

However the Programme still had to turn its First Taste of Power into full-on control. It had many influential enemies and many detractors, who, as always with new Programmes, underrated it. Cameron resigned after the defeat, but was not replaced with a populist Brexiter but with Theresa May, a former 'Remain' supporter. Pro-EU activists took to the streets, with huge marches in London. Political Success was by no means guaranteed for the Programme.

It rose to the challenge – that's what true Political Programmes do. Mrs May hoped to counteract it and aim for a deal with Europe, but she found herself pressurized by her party into taking an ever-tougher approach. During the referendum, various models of life outside the EU had been mooted. Norway was part of the EU single market. Turkey was part of the customs union. Switzerland was part of the Schengen Zone (free movement across borders). The new Programme, now in full cry, would have none of these compromises. Its aim was a 'hard' Brexit, cutting the UK off from Europe as much as possible.

Some commentators remain puzzled by why Mrs May fell in line with this: she seems to have ditched all her previous beliefs. But such is the power of a Political Programme cresting a rising Zeitgeist. Her party was flocking round the new banner, and she had little choice to do otherwise. Her time in office is best seen as a series of attempted compromise solutions, aimed at halting the rising 'hard Brexit' tide, which simply flooded past them, obliterating them like sandcastles. Mrs May was Queen Canute.

Her attempts ended after disastrous (for her) European Election results in May 2019, where the Conservatives were virtually wiped out. 29 of the 73 seats went to the Brexit Party, Farage's reinvention of UKIP. She resigned, tearfully, and the Conservatives chose Boris Johnson to take over – as they had to: he was the charismatic Leader that the rising Programme needed.

This was a Palace Revolution, the first such revolution in this story not to have happened during a war. It was carried out with the ruthlessness associated with such events, with the party purging itself of Europhiles.

This was another step forward for the Programme. Now, what it really needed was a Great Endorsement. In December 2019, it got one. Labour and the Lib Dems have been criticized for letting the 'Christmas election' happen. It made little sense if one looked at the polls. But the country had to be asked if it really did want Brexit, not through another referendum but through the proper method of establishing public desire in a representative democracy, a general election. It delivered its answer, Johnson winning an 80-seat Landslide. This surprised many people, but fits perfectly with the model outlined in this book. The new-look Conservatives had an original Big Idea that caught the mood of the times and enough of a Political Programme built round it.

Some people deny this, and say that the Brexit movement did not have a constellation of Models, Values and Polices around its Big Idea – it was just a Slogan that got lucky. Where were the impressive political minds that have given rise to all the other Programmes in this story? This is unfair – and unwise. There was limited academic support for Brexit, but there was some, for example from economist Patrick Minford and historian Robert Tombs. Nigel Farage had a true entrepreneur's passion and communicated it powerfully. Dominic Cummings and Matthew Elliott of Vote Leave were serious thinkers – yes, they were mavericks, but Programmes in their infancy need mavericks. It is a classic mistake of failing old Programmes to underrate the leading figures in rising ones. This seems to have been particularly acute in this case.

At the same time, Brexit did not have the intellectual roots of the great Programmes, and this is now showing. Its Second Story was not thought through – or rather it was thought through, but Brexiters came to wildly different conclusions, which they never thrashed out. Like Lloyd George's 1916 Programme, it was all First Story. 'Get Brexit done!' Then what? This weakness would come home to haunt the Programme.

But in 2019, that was for the future. The Great Endorsement of the new Programme was Waterloo for the residual liberalism of both New Labour and the Coalition, who were suddenly the bad guys in the new populist world. The old Programme's supporters tumbled into classic, ill-natured Dissolution-phase factionalism. For example, JK Rowling, creator of the emblematic Harry Potter series, found herself under vicious attack from fellow progressives over her views on trans rights.

What did the victorious new Programme look like? Its essential Models were a view of society divided in two, with 'the people' on one side (decent, hard-working, patriotic) and 'the elite' on the other (self-serving, arrogant, out-of-touch). Its geopolitics was all about competing nation states: forget transnational bodies. There was an expressed belief in the importance of Cultural Power (Gramsci was no doubt turning in his grave). Many Conservative Brexiters added libertarian, small-state economics, but kept quiet about this on the campaign trail.

Its Values were those of Populism: 'common sense' (as defined by the right), nationalism, anti-elitism.

The Programme's Core Policy was a hard Brexit. Allied to that was a Culture War against elite complacency and 'wokeness'. Foreign policy became about ignoring Europe and 'tilting' to the Indo-Pacific area. Johnson talked of levelling up the North and South of the country, though advocates of the small state wondered how that would be paid for.

Its Stories? There was a long list of Villains. The liberal metropolitan elite. The BBC. Experts of all kinds, but particularly judges. 'Woke' activists. Immigrants (not demonized as openly as the rest, but once in power, the Programme was eager to keep as many out as possible). The arch-Villain, based in its towering, glass-fronted, foreign headquarters, was the European Commission.

Ranged against this villainy was the Archetype: Workington Man, an older, white, male, skilled working-class town-dweller. He was not ambitious culturally or career-wise, unlike the eager Wilsonian technocrat, the aspirational Thatcherite entrepreneur or the intellectually curious metropolitan Blairite. He was proud of his country and angry at austerity, at what he believed to be the effects of immigration – job losses for locals and overstretched public services – and at being talked down to by London-based decision-makers.

The Second Story? That was where things went wrong. The reality of Brexit was always that it would be costly, in the short term at least. Trade with mainland Europe would suffer, and even with a rush of new trade deals, it would take exporters years to conquer new markets. Those exporters still trying to do business with Europe would suffer from added paperwork and would lose business to EU-based competitors. Massive amounts of money would need to be spent on training Brits to fill the job vacancies left by departing Europeans. European projects such as the Galileo satellite system, whose costs were spread across many nations, would have to be replicated and funded by us alone. However the Programme had presented Brexit to the electorate as a cost-cutting exercise, with an extra £350 million a week suddenly available to boost the NHS.

And then there was the fundamental disagreement about what kind of Britain the Brexiters wanted. One wing of the party, led by Johnson, wanted to spend, spend, spend, on infrastructure, on levelling up, on creating a 'high-wage' economy.

The other wing had a diametrically opposite vision. They wanted a small, lean state, freeing up business which would then generate huge growth to pay for any of these bills. They had their own Sacred Text, *Britannia Unchained*, written in 2012 by five, then fresh-faced and obscure MPs: Liz Truss, Kwasi Kwarteng, Dominic Raab, Priti Patel and Chris Skidmore.

The book celebrated libertarian economics, low taxation and deregulation. Its Model of both international and human relations was one where ruthless competition prevailed. Its Values? Enterprise. Education – of a very specific kind: the basics to start with, later specialization in maths and the sciences (the arts got little mention, apart from complaints that too many youngsters wasted their energies studying them). Above all, it valued simple hard work: personal and national success came from graft. British workers, the book said, had not been good at this of late. Instead, we were 'among the worst idlers in the world'. This vision became known as Singapore-on-Thames. Despite Johnson, who was naturally suspicious of ideology, it soon became the dominant force in the party. Various think-tanks sprung up to support it, many of them based in a Tufton Street townhouse provided for them by a wealthy well-wisher.

The Cultural Endorsement of the Programme? There was a new mood of proud nostalgia, as the nation celebrated the 'going it alone' spirit of the Second World War on the 75th anniversaries of D-Day and VE Day in 2019 and 2020. We all cheered as 99-year-old War veteran Tom Moore paced up and down his front garden to raise money for the NHS. A tone of earthy, confident contrarianism was set by the Programme's Leaders, Farage and Johnson.

The actual creators of culture, however, were not very enthusiastic. High culture is an elite business, so was on the wrong side of the barricades. Popular culture is largely produced by young people, who didn't vote for Brexit anyway (though a few old wild men of rock came out in favour of it: Ringo Starr, Roger Daltrey, The Fall's Mark E Smith).

The Programme responded to this lack of enthusiasm by launching a US-style 'Culture War' against those unresponsive elites and 'woke' youngsters. This included appointing Nadine Dorries, author of popular paperbacks set in 1950s Liverpool, as Culture Secretary. The party faithful rallied to the flag, but much of the rest of the population found Culture War unnecessarily strident and (fatal for a nationalist Programme) not really, well, British. And in the end, you win a Culture War by producing superior culture, culture that moves and excites people, that makes them envision their lives in new, relevant and impassioned ways. Repeats of *Dad's Army* (delightful as they are) just won't cut it.

The Counterblasts, by contrast, flourished. My own personal favourite is Jonathan Coe's novel *Middle England*, which takes a caring and funny look at a nation drowning in irate retrospection. Internationally, the mindset of nationalism was challenged by organizations like Global Citizen. Online, young people have a culture where they make friends and game with peers from all round the world. While they are at ease with gentle nationalism, they enjoy diversity.

The Programme had its first Big Win on 31st January 2020, when Britain formally left the EU.

A Crowning Glory to go with that Win? England's successful run to the final in the delayed UEFA Euro 2020 men's football championships saw Number Ten draped in St George's flags. But this wasn't 30th July 1966. England lost the game by the narrowest of margins, a penalty shoot-out after extra time. And even if our penalties had gone in, the success of the diverse team and its thoughtful manager Gareth Southgate belonged to a different world than that of the Programme. When the players took the knee before each game to protest against racism, they attracted negative comment from some Programme-supporting MPs, boos from racists in the crowd and ever more convoluted refusals from Johnson to explicitly condemn that booing. Yes, our run to the final and our sympathy for the young men put on the line in the penalty shoot-out did unite the country – but not in a way the Programme wanted.

In 2022 our women's team went one better and won the trophy. But by that time the Programme was already in trouble. The bunting went up again at Number Ten but Johnson didn't attend the final – unlike his losing counterpart, German's Olaf Scholz – possibly because he feared booing from the crowd. That is not the stuff of Crowning Glories, where Programme Leaders bask gleefully in a new national mood.

Supporters of the Programme can argue that it was denied a proper Crowning Glory by the pandemic.

On the very day of the Programme's first Big Win, exiting the EU, the first cases of the Covid-19 virus were announced in the UK. This was a terrifying threat, way beyond the playbook of any administration in this story (Lloyd George's second Programme had muddled through the Spanish flu, the nature of which was not understood at the time). So, one should not be hyper-critical: would any administration have dealt with this with aplomb?

But… The Programme reacted slowly, despite getting warning from events in Italy. Johnson didn't bother to attend vital COBRA meetings, then flouted medical advice by pointedly shaking hands with people to show what he thought of experts. It nearly got him killed. Supplies of personal protective equipment (PPE) were inadequate, and a trumpeted 'world-beating' test and trace system (typical of a newly-endorsed Programme to be this boastful) turned out to be expensive and not very effective. Britain soon had one of the highest *per capita* case levels in the world. Yet, because of the uniquely horrifying nature of the virus, there was only limited public anger about these things – a classic Great Escape.

The pandemic even gave the Programme a Big Win. Once it was announced that a vaccine was being trialled, a Vaccine Taskforce was set up under businesswoman Kate Bingham. This proved highly effective. The success of the UK vaccine rollout was particularly pleasing for the Programme, as its arch-villain in Brussels was inept in trying to do the same thing, entering late into the vaccine market then stamping its little foot when it didn't get exactly what it wanted.

Another Big Win came from the massive support system for businesses forced to close due to lockdown, and yet another would come in 2022, from the Programme's staunch support of Ukraine after Russia's invasion – again, in contrast to some hesitancy across the channel.

It looked as if the Programme's Pomp would continue for a while, but Slow Stranglers were at work.

One was the simple fact that Brexit wasn't working. The inevitable costs, outlined earlier, began to kick in – and the Programme had no answer to them. Where was the promised flood of trade deals? Where were all the newly-trained Brits ready to take over from all those continentals who had been pricing them out of work? Why were many businesses having to do more paperwork, not less? What was actually going to be done about the Irish border? Estimates of lost business began to trickle in: 4% from the Office of Budget Responsibility, 5.5% from the (admittedly pro-Europe but highly respected) Centre for European Reform…

A more obviously visible Strangler was a series of scandals and the administration's self-serving responses. The first was the Dominic Cummings affair. Johnson's special adviser flouted the lockdown rules in April 2020 with his ill-advised trip to Barnard Castle, but when this became public a month later, Johnson refused to sack him. Next, a former minister, Owen Paterson, was found guilty of having breached lobbying rules. Again, rather than following the usual course of suspending him, the administration tried to force through changes in those rules in order to exonerate him. "One rule for them, another for us," people muttered.

Then came 'Partygate'… Johnson was revealed to have held parties at Number Ten during the lockdown period, while ordinary citizens had been unable to visit relatives, even dying ones. The parties were officially denied, then admitted but made light of. The public mood, stoical and largely forgiving during the pandemic itself, changed. This became the Programme's First Big Failure, creating a large dent in its popularity, but not in itself undermining its core ideology of populist anti-Europeanism.

Johnson toughed this out, but was eventually forced from office by a lesser scandal, 'Pinchergate'. The Deputy Chief Whip was accused of groping men at the Carlton Club. This time, Johnson dismissed him – but, true to form, lied about having known about Pincher's having done this before. This proved one falsehood too much for the PM's colleagues. A tsunami of resignations propelled him from office in early July – though he refused to relinquish the Prime Ministership until a replacement was elected.

Johnson had skilfully managed to paper over the Big Split in the party, between the spenders (his own team) and 'Singapore-on-Thames'. The moment he left, this split became painfully apparent. The battle to replace him turned into a contest between the two wings. On September 7th, the party members voted for the latter one and its candidate, Liz Truss.

She sprang into action at once, appointing fellow *Britannia Unchained* author Kwarteng as her Chancellor. The expert Permanent Secretary to the Treasury, Sir Tom Scholar, was fired. A budget was quickly announced, but called a 'fiscal event' to avoid the need to run its assumptions past more experts at the Office of Budget Responsibility. The event took place on 23rd September. There would be huge tax cuts to stimulate a dash for growth (where had we heard that term before?) This would be paid for from borrowing. 'At last!' proclaimed the *Daily Mail*, 'A True Tory Budget!'

Was this the real triumph of the Programme? Had the free-spending Johnson actually been a barrier to its proper fulfilment, which was using what Truss called 'the freedoms of Brexit' to shrink the state and create Singapore-on-Thames?

If so, it was extraordinarily short-lived. Global investors responded in horror, ditching pounds and UK bonds so aggressively that the rate at which we could borrow shot up from under 2% to nearly 4% within a week. The Bank of England, afraid that the pensions industry would collapse, piled into the markets and hiked domestic interest rates. Truss sacked Kwarteng. Her new Chancellor, Jeremy Hunt, reversed almost all the changes in the 'fiscal event'. Markets calmed down. Truss resigned shortly afterwards, the shortest-lasting Prime Minister in UK history. In a new election (in which MPs made sure that party members took no part), the pragmatic Rishi Sunak became PM. He is a classic Replacement Leader.

The fiasco of the 44-day Truss premiership was the Body-blow for the Programme. It was oddly similar to 'Black Wednesday' of 16th September

1992, when global markets destroyed the credibility of what was left of the Thatcherite Programme. Gone was its Cultural Power. Before the fiasco, it was rare to hear any official or semi-official voices criticizing Brexit. Now it is a regular occurrence (though Labour is still unwilling to join them). The party has huge deficits in the polls. Other polls show deep regret about Brexit, with only the over-65s still thinking it was a good idea.

Also as in 1992, the Conservatives remain in power, but the Programme is now limping along. It remains split, not just two ways but three. The Singapore-on-Thames advocates haven't gone away, though I imagine they are looking for new leaders. The Johnsonites have already started arguing that only 'Boris' can get the public vote. There are still no gains from Brexit in sight. And recently the administration has started announcing new policies out of nowhere – suddenly all children will have to study maths till they're 18, even if they can't stand the subject. That is a sure sign of a rudderless, broken Programme.

A new Zeitgeist is now driving the nation to look for fresh ideas, fresh leadership. Where will that come from?

Populist 'Brexit' Nationalism

Provisional Leader: Nigel Farage

Leader: Boris Johnson

Replacement Leaders: Liz Truss, Rishi Sunak

Core Policies: Hard Brexit, Culture War, (for one wing) 'Singapore-on-Thames', (for the other wing) infrastructure and levelling up

Crucible Groups: Bruges Group, ERG

Action Groups: Anti-Federalist League, Vote Leave, Leave.eu

Sacred Text: Margaret Thatcher's Bruges Speech, (for Singapore-on-Thames wing) *Britannia Unchained*

Villains: The liberal metropolitan elite, the BBC, experts, 'woke' students/commentators, EU immigrants, asylum seekers

Arch-Villain: The European Commission

Archetype: Workington Man

Bright Future: Britain a 'world-beating' nation again

Significant Influence: Cameron promises referendum in 2013

First Taste of Power: 2016 referendum

Great Endorsement: 2019 Christmas election

Cultural Endorsement: The Programme-supporting press, the patriotic mood on 75th anniversaries of key WW2 events

Counterblasts: Jonathan Coe *Middle England*, Global Citizen

Crowning Glory (delayed): Reaching the finals of Euro 2020

Great Escapes: Early responses to Covid-19, boasts about test and trace

Big Wins: Formally quitting EU, Vaccine rollout, support for Ukraine

Slow Stranglers: Failure of Brexit policies, 'One rule for them…'

First Big Failure: 'Partygate' revelations

Big Split: Johnsonian spenders vs. Singapore-on-Thames

Body-blow: Global response to Truss/Kwarteng 'Fiscal Event'

2024: A New Deal?
A Speculation

The collapse of the Populist Brexit Nationalist Programme has left an open goal for Labour. Yet that party still seems to have no real Programme. At an event in mid-2022, Sir Kier Starmer said that what he wanted to do was 'fix things'. When asked what his biggest priority was, he replied that it was growth (which, at the time, was exactly the same as the Conservatives'). Europe? Ancient history. So no 'Blue Ocean' there. Yet as I sit here writing this, his party has a massive lead in the polls. Is this not a Popperian refutation of my model? Here is a party with no apparent desire to create a distinctive Political Programme (by my definition) and it is heading for a Landslide!

Well… Firstly, poll leads two years before a scheduled election are one thing; actually winning that election by a Landslide is another. Secondly, there is time for a genuine progressive Political Programme to develop. Thirdly, supporters of Starmer argue that he does have a Programme, similar in tone to that of Stanley Baldwin. Tranquillity. 'Safety First.'

I accept the first two arguments but not the third. There seems to be a genuine lack of vision on the left, an excess of caution spooked by the losses of 'Red Wall' seats in the North of England – once unwisely overlooked voters who are now having too much attention lavished on them.

Is there a rising mood that would encourage more courageous thinking? I believe that there is, though it still needs a Crucible Group and a Leader to turn its outlines and emotions into a true Political Programme.

So far, this book has been strictly factual, plus a bit of personal interpretation. However, I feel it is now necessary to wing out and speculate. What might a 2020s Progressive Political Programme look and feel like? Above all, I feel, it must be innovative and proud of it. "We are going to do things differently."

Models

It would need to have, and proudly trumpet, new Models. It needs a fresh *vision of the state* as an active and essential creator of value. This means challenging Public Choice Theory and, instead, creating new Models of how public services can be run efficiently and enthusiastically. There is, I imagine, a huge range of opportunities for using technology to achieve this. I envisage nerdy Technosocialists debating these with the passion that early Thatcherites had for ways of measuring Money Supply.

My guess is that this will lead to less outsourcing. The new public services will do more 'in house', and do so with pride. At the same time, there still need to be ways of involving genuinely innovative, value-creating outsiders in the adventure of public service.

Concepts in *economics* that were swept aside in the torrent of neo-liberalism, such as market failure, public goods and the protection of commons, need to be taken seriously again.

It's interesting to note that the old Thatcher/Reagan enthusiasm for 'supply side' macroeconomics is being revisited both by Labour in the UK and the Democrats in the US, with a new focus on the economic benefits of childcare provision, mass retraining and support for small business.

A Progressive Programme must face up fully to the seriousness of

Climate Change. To do so, it will need a robust, accurate, science-based Model of the ecological threats to the planet and what needs to be done in response to them. The best I know are provided by the Stockholm Resilience Centre, who have identified nine major threats to our future, quantified them (some are more pressing than others) and come up with thresholds beyond which we are really entering the danger zone.

I also sense the need for a new Model of human *psychology*. The authors of *Britannia Unchained* regarded us as rational, ruthless maximizers of individual economic utility, with one major addition, that we also do this for our families (a second addition, perhaps, is that we have a sense of patriotism). By contrast, Progressive Programmes such as New Liberalism or the Roy Jenkins wing of 'White Heat' had a much broader view of humanity, informed as much by literature and the arts as economics and ethology. Its psychology was humanistic.

Perhaps the best-known Model in the humanistic tradition is Abraham Maslow's *Hierarchy of Needs*. In this, we work hard to meet basic needs such as food and shelter, then move on to more abstract ones such as belonging and, ultimately, self-actualization. This might sound hideously egocentric, but Maslow's self-actualizers are givers not takers: they are creative, co-operative, curious, generous, big-hearted and empathetic. They contribute to the wider good. Struggles at the base of Maslow's Hierarchy may be zero-sum games – though our ancestors hunted and gathered in groups, not as individuals – but the ones at the top are definitely not. Translating this into politics, the ideal society is one where basic needs are met and as many people as possible grow to their full potential, at which point they will enrich society in a myriad different ways. Sound familiar? Back in 1905, this was the view of the New Liberals.

The current Programme has an all-against-all model of geopolitics, too: a world of competing, irreconcilable national interests. Time for a new Model of *international relations* that clearly and logically demonstrates the benefits of international co-operation.

Values

In its Values, a Progressive Political Programme must offer something more compelling than 'growth', or even 'sustainable growth'. Labour have started talking about a 'fairer, greener future', which is a good start, but they still seem very calm about it all. We reveal our true Values through our emotions. Anger at violations of them: where is the simple rage at food banks in a first-world country or at the continuing ignoring, in some quarters, of the threat of Climate Change? Excitement at their expression and realization: where is the buzz around creating a kinder, safer, better-run, more magnanimous country?

Given the new, positive vision of the state, the Programme would once more celebrate *public service*, a deep desire to use one's energies in the service of others. The 2022 Christmas speech by King Charles III was brimming over with such celebration. People with this Value do not have to work in the public sector, though many, no doubt, will. When teaching business, I met many students eager to work in the private sector but determined to ensure that their work was socially useful as well as profitable.

Expert knowledge would be valued again. People who have spent years studying a subject will be listened to with respect, not sacked on a new leader's arrival in office. *Intelligence* would be admired, not scoffed at for having been acquired in an 'ivory tower' or making people 'too clever by half'. Why not invite expert non-politicians into government, a policy trialled by Gordon Brown when he created a 'government of all the

186

talents' in 2007? (Maybe the acronym used at the time, GOAT, could be dropped…) Government will be seen as an art again. Maybe the best of our leaders will earn the title 'statesman' or 'stateswoman'.

Yes, this is elitist, but the country needs to be led by the brightest and most able. Nothing less will do, in these tough times. In return for the privilege of authority, leaders would be obliged to explain their policies *clearly* and in detail to the rest of us. I believe that voters are bored with soundbites and bar-room know-it-alls, and want to have their intelligence respected.

We have certainly had enough of being lied to. A commitment to *truthfulness* would be at the heart of the new Programme's promise – which would be backed up by the dismissal of anyone found falling short of that standard.

Creativity would be another core value. Not just the creativity of artists, but of planners, scientists and entrepreneurs. Faced with its current problems, the nation – and the world – needs, above all, new thought, new ideas, new technologies, new solutions.

There would be a celebration of *diversity*. Ethnic, sexual and, beyond this, a Jenkinsian sense that people have a right to choose their own path and not be dragged off it. (To be fair to the current Programme, it front bench is more ethnically diverse than the opposition's, even though some of those front-benchers don't seem very keen on letting more diversity into the country.)

The Programme would be *international* in outlook The world's – and thus, in the long term, our – biggest problems are transnational, and cannot be sorted at a national level. Yet the modern world is a dangerous place.

Liberal, or even moderately liberal, democracy is under physical, not just ideological threat, in a way it wasn't a decade ago. War, surely, must be avoided – the consequences would be horrific. Getting this balance, between standing up for our Values while avoiding outright war, will require statesmanship, expertise and skill. Thank heavens those things will be respected again.

Finally, bringing things gently home – a quiet but heartfelt core Value would be simple *care for others*. A model based on selfishness ultimately just grinds people down. The poor get poorer and the rich ever more complicit. Time to move on. Compassion isn't soft; it has a strong, active, life-sustaining energy.

Stories

There would be plenty of *Heroes*. Experts of all kinds. Scientists. Skilled, committed leaders and public servants. Green business-people (especially entrepreneurs). Artists. Carers. Thoughtful regulators, protecting us from dodgy business-people and climate-abusers while minimizing unnecessary interference. *Villains?* Those dodgy business-people, climate-abusers and their apologists. Overseas, strongman enemies of liberal democracy.

The *Victims* in need of Rescue? The disadvantaged. The different. The next generation. The planet.

Who will be the *Archetype*? Maybe it's time it was a 'she'. A nurse? Certainly a public servant of some kind. She will be feisty – nobody's doormat – but with a strong caring side. She'd be interested in the world, always wanting to find out more, and angry about the damage done to the planet that is being left to her children. Her two children? Why not? At the local comp, doing their best. One of them has real artistic talent, and she's fiercely proud of that…

Core Policies

The current ogre is the cost of living. Debate continues on the best way to tackle that: the new Programme will need to find policies here that both work and suit their overall Values.

Beyond this, policies will be needed for rebuilding the public sector, for truly tackling the problem of mental health, for boosting productivity (the UK is one of the least efficient countries in Europe), for education and reskilling (a huge task), for repairing our relationship with the rest of Europe, and for keeping peace in a dangerous world.

But above all, a Progressive Programme will need to tackle Climate Change. This can't be done just by negative measures: taxing flights, discouraging car use (etc.) The Emergency must, in its own way, be seen in a positive light. If it is a threat, it is also an opportunity for imagination, creativity and entrepreneurship. Labour is currently talking about a 'Green Industrial Revolution' – but not exactly at the top of its voice. The new Programme will shout this, or something similar, from the rooftops, and new voters will respond favourably.

Other aspects

Sacred Texts. Go deep: the great Programmes do. Thomas Piketty, Mariana Mazzucato, Kate Raworth (in late December, relax, sit down and reread *A Christmas Carol*). But there is a gap here. The Programme needs its own version of Jenkins' *The Labour Case* or, best of all, its own Beveridge Report. Get writing, progressives!

The cost. Taxation would have to rise to pay for these policies, but our overall quality of life, with better healthcare, education (etc.), safer streets and a sustainable planet would rise even more.

The Metrics. Some objective measure of that quality will need to be established, as ultimately that is what the Programme promises and so must be judged by. GDP will not be sufficient. Gross National Happiness? Why not? As long as the metric is clear and can't be fudged.

Its Culture. The young – or a critical mass of them, anyway – have no truck with racism, sexism or homophobia. They care deeply about ecological threats – it's their future. At the same time, they are not technophobes: they respect, use and enjoy technology. They celebrate their lives – culture is about joy, as well as Values – at communal events like festivals and gigs, which often feature music from around the world (Jeremy Corbyn even got his name chanted at Glastonbury in 2017: he has not turned out to be the right Leader for this Programme, but the enthusiasm was there). This culture is vibrant; it is time for progressive politicians to engage with it. New votes are here, aplenty, waiting to be won by the right politicians with the right message.

Freedom matters in this culture. While the progressive state must enable, it can't be too bossy. A paradox? Clear thinking – and a convincing Leader – should overcome this. It's about deeply respecting individual choice but drawing lines, intelligently and passionately, around areas where that choice fails to deliver ethically acceptable outcomes. Currently the right seems to have cornered the market in messages about freedom. This narrative needs reclaiming. This would, surely, not be difficult. The sum total of human freedom is clearly expanded in a well-run, empowering state and is diminished in one where poverty blights many lives – as, again, the New Liberals understood over a century ago.

What would be *carried forward* from the old Programme? A diverse front bench. Support for Ukraine. A Johnsonian enthusiasm for tech: the Programme could even recreate Harold Wilson's Ministry of Technology. Patriotism must be reclaimed – you can be proud of being British and want close ties with Europe. Why not, if such ties mean greater peace and greater prosperity?

What *Big Battle* must it fight? My guess is the fossil fuel industry and lobby, and, behind them, all the people who deprioritize 'Net Zero' and other Climate-related policies.

Finally, what would the *Big Idea* be? The simple phrase that sums it all up? It's not hugely original, but the idea of a 21st Century New Deal won't go away. Of course, that would set the bar for originality high – but that's what we need now.

The Idea's *elevator pitch*? How about: 'We will put our brightest and best minds to work on finding creative and co-operative solutions to our problems. An enabling state will play a key part in this, creating public goods such as education, mental/physical health and a fair society, and protecting common goods – especially the survival of the planet. To pay for this, taxes will have to rise, but our quality of life will rise even more.'

The last few pages might seem excessively idealistic – but so do most Political Programmes in their infancy (and when they lose their idealism, they wither). And, as I said, they are just speculation. I didn't write this book to second-guess the future, a task I believe to be impossible. I wrote it to show how futures get created, and, OK, to spend a little time hinting at a direction that future-builders might constructively follow.

A New Deal?

Models

      The state as enabler

      Economics revisited

      Rigorous understanding of the ecological threats

      Humanistic psychology

      A co-operative Model of international relations

Values

      Fairness

      Public service

      Expertise / intelligence

      Clarity

      Telling the truth

      Creativity

      Diversity

      Internationalism

      Care

      Personal freedom (reclaiming the narrative)

Core Policies on...

      Climate Change

      Inflation / cost of living

      Inequality (especially mental health)

      A revitalized public sector

      Productivity

      Education

      Europe

Metric

      Quality of life

Conclusion

In the spirit of Popper and Lakatos I should end by making some predictions by which this book and its model can be judged.

The first is that the Truss/Kwarteng fiasco was a true Body-blow. The current Programme is now broken and will lose the next election.

That's not exactly Nostradamus, so I shall add to that prediction. If Labour does not articulate a vision for the future that is substantially more compelling than their current one, that election will be close. If there were an election tomorrow (I'm writing this in early 2023), the polls say it would result in a Labour Landslide. But the election isn't scheduled until late 2024. Without a genuine Aspirant Political Programme ranged against them, the Conservatives will claw back much of their current losses.

If that happens, a 1970s-style sense of Drift will continue until a new Political Programme arises.

At some time, however, one *will* arise. One of the parties will catch (and partially drive) a new mood in the nation. It will come up with a fresh, clear Big Idea, that has thought-through Models, Values, Stories and Core Policies constellated around it. There will be a Leader who believes deeply in these and conveys that belief with passion. It will stir the hearts and minds of a section of the electorate – especially a previously overlooked one or a new one (the young) – so that they say "Yes!" and feel that politics is, after all, for them. Then, and only then, will a Landslide result.

Will this be a Progressive Programme? That I can't say. You've no doubt guessed that I would like to see that. I've even suggested one in the previous section. But there is no guarantee that this suggestion, or anything remotely like it, will triumph.

This is not purely a matter of fate, however. If progressives want to see their ideas and people in the driving seat, they must do what they can to nudge the spirit of the age their direction and create an Aspirant Political Programme that captures that emerging spirit in courageous, creative and compelling ways. The story of the last 120 years shows this can be done.

A crisis is also a time of opportunity.

Four Predictions

This is the end of the line for the current Programme. It will lose the next election...

...But if the alternative is not a full-on Political Programme, with fresh (and clearly stated) Models, Values, Core Polices constellated round a fresh (and clearly stated) Big Idea, it will not lose by much.

Politics will then go into a period of Drift, until...

...A fully-fledged Aspirant Political Programme is presented to the electorate. This will win a Landslide victory.

Ten Quick Tips for the Ambitious

Here are ten key points for anyone seeking to create a Political Programme.

1. Don't Triangulate, Innovate
A Political Programme emerges from a new way of looking at the
world, a new set of priorities. Your job is to impassion people, and
you won't do this by simply rebadging or recombining old stuff.
Choose the battlegrounds: create a Blue Ocean.

2. Stand on the Shoulders of Giants
Study deep thinkers. Thatcherism was inspired by Nobel
Prizewinners. Don't be shy about this. To turn their lofty ideas
into practical policies…

3. Start with a Brilliant Crucible Group
Assemble a group of like-minded but diverse individuals, and thrash
out your Worldview, Core Policies and Big Idea. Cast the net wide,
beyond just your party.

4. Tell Powerful Stories
Think of those tribal elders entrancing their young around a fire on
a starlit night. What is the evil Dragon? How will you slay it? What
Bright Future will you build once it is slain? How will you do this?

5. Ride the Wave
Does the spirit of these Stories chime with the *Zeitgeist*, with rising
concerns and values in culture (especially popular culture)?
Catch this wave – then help build it, too.

6. Have the Right Leader

This person must have an intuitive connection with a wide swathe of voters – 'your people' – and with the emerging era. They must be PM material. You have such a person? Remember Lloyd George in 1918/22: it's not just about one individual.

7. Be Thick-Skinned

Remember, too, that Sir Keith Joseph, arguably the leading intellectual force behind Thatcherism, was nicknamed 'the mad monk' by his colleagues in the early 1970s.

8. Be Patient

The *Zeitgeist* moves in a mysterious way. If your ideas are strong and you keep fighting for them, their time should come. The Brexiters began their campaign in the late 1980s, doubled their support in Winter 2012/3, and achieved their Great Endorsement in 2019.

9. Understand your (Internal) Rivals' Neediness

If you have truly (and finally!) caught the public mood, you offer your party colleagues what they crave most: office. Once you convince them this is true, they (or enough of them) will bury their old hatchets and rally round you. In the early 1960s, Labour stopped squabbling and came together (enough) to support White Heat.

10. Do not Compromise any Key Programme Elements for Quick Wins as you gain Influence

This is a particular danger for an Aspirant Programme offered a Taste of Power in a coalition. The 'Orange Book' Liberals paid the ultimate electoral price by agreeing to raise student loans.

Appendix A
Some Critiques of My Model

I want to look at three possible criticisms of the model (and of this book generally).

1. It's Got its Head in the Clouds'

This objection is that all this talk of Programmes, vision, creativity, Blue Oceans (etc.) sounds fine, but is really only for politics nuts like me or, seeing as you have got this far in the book, you. Voters, this objection runs, are interested in more basic stuff – health, education, housing, prices, jobs, law enforcement, national security – and how to provide these most efficiently.

There is some truth in that, -- but only some. Ultimately, this argument belittles voters. We all have Values, and Political Programmes capture changes in these that are felt deeply by many, many people. That's what makes Programmes so special – and so successful. The historical section of this book, I hope, has demonstrated this.

The argument had its heyday back in the 1990s. After the Cold War, some people began claiming that the time of 'Big Picture' debates was over. They talked of 'The End of History'. We know how to run complex modern economies, they said. From now on, the debate will just be about who could do so most effectively.

The financial crisis of 2007/8 sank the 'we know how to run things' argument. We clearly do *not* know, and the debate on how to organize society continues.

We don't even 'know' what sort of society we want. Do we want an 'enterprise' society where the feckless and stupid go to the wall? A 'protective' society where everyone gets looked after (but, maybe, where bright outliers get bored and where cynics triumph by gaming the system)? Something in between? If so, what, exactly? How authoritarian do we want government to be? The world is fast dividing into two camps on this issue. And so on.

If there is an absolute certainty in the modern world (unless you are on the far right or work for the PR department of a fossil fuel company) it is Climate Change. But what are the right actions in the light of it?

High-level political debate is alive, kicking and necessary. History has not ended; it is rushing on, changing ever faster.

2. It's Interesting History, but the Future will be Radically Different

A contrary objection is not that my model is too ambitious, but that it is not ambitious enough. The material in this book is all well and good, but politics has irrevocably changed. It's nice to read about Baldwin with his pipe or Tony Blair's grin – but the future is online, and online is a jungle where carnivores like Donald Trump prowl. The old rules of polite debate have been swept away. The election process itself is under attack. Voters are being herded into extreme bubbles by tech platforms. Welcome to a 'post-truth' world.

Politeness

It's an illusion that debate was always polite in the past, as anyone familiar with the works of James Gillray or Thomas Rowlandson will attest. And we still have rules today. If people overstep them, they do themselves more harm than good. Recently, the expletive-laden emails sent by Gavin Williamson led to his dismissal.

The process is under attack

This objection carries more sway in America than in the UK. Over there, there does seem to be a genuine assault on the mechanisms of democracy. A relentless stream of propaganda continues to deny the result of the 2020 election. Election officials have been harassed or dismissed. Rules are being put in place that make it harder for poor people to vote.

But Americans are fighting back. The predicted 'Red Landslide' in the November 2022 mid-term elections did not materialize, and election-denying candidates were particularly punished. People in the US value their democracy, and won't be bullied or cheated out of it.

Bubblification

(I don't know if that's a real word, but it sounds good.) The algorithms of the giant tech platforms push users to extremes, not out of conspiracy or malice but to make money: extremes create bubbles and people in bubbles are more predictable and thus easier to sell to. Because the algorithms have no understanding of content, they create political and ideological bubbles as well as consumer ones. Once inside them, we get an unending feed of stuff from other extremists. This 'normalizes' such extremism and moves the centre of gravity of debate.

Will this be fatal to democracy? The sad answer is that it might be. However we are getting cagier. Social media are a new phenomenon, which essentially caught us unawares. The younger generation is much more aware of the unreliability of online content. We do not like being herded by machines. I expect a fight back against this, too.

A 'post-truth' world

Truth does not prosper in bubbles. Again, this is scary, but in the long run, I trust people to resist lies. Boris Johnson was brought down because his associates got fed up with his 'post-truth' attitudes.

Truth is not a 'nice to have', but a core part of being a sane human being. To live in a world of lies is madness, as Freud, for whom the 'reality principle' was the guarantor of sanity, understood. We will, ultimately, fight for truth because we need it to survive psychologically.

A more sinister version of this objection is that lying will become ever more sophisticated, so that ultimately even the most valiant warrior for truth simply won't be able to tell truth from fiction. Recently I watched

202

an episode of the TV series *The Capture* where a government minister gave a speech on mainstream TV that was totally at variance with his previously expressed beliefs – and we saw the minister watching it, horrified; the speech was being given by an avatar. (Or, of course, I could have turned the TV off and simply picked up Orwell's *1984*.)

This is indeed terrifying, but we are not there yet. I believe that my model, which is based on the ability of voters to think for themselves, remains valid.

3. Life doesn't fit Models

Every model-builder of human affairs knows this one. The answer is: 'Of course life doesn't fit models, not fully, but model-building is the only way we can make sense of the world'.

Models in the 'hard' sciences like Physics and Chemistry aspire to perfection. Maybe they can achieve it: no exception has yet been found to the Periodic Table of the Elements. But in human and social affairs, models have to find a humbler place in what is called Thorngate's Impostulate. This is a triangle where one corner is *Accuracy*, another is *Simplicity*, and the third is breadth of application (or *'Generalizability'*).

Accurate

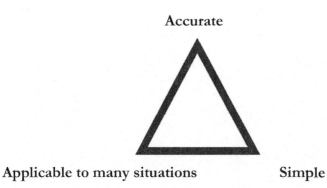

Applicable to many situations   **Simple**

If you want perfection (or near-perfection) in one direction, there will be trade-offs in one or two of the others. The most ambitious models go for a high level of accuracy plus one of the other two desiderata, breadth and simplicity. Karl Marx, for example, believed his model to be totally accurate and reckoned it was universally generalizable, applying to all human history. Simple? No: *Das Kapital* contains 300,000 words of dense prose. An Ordinance Survey map, by contrast, is scrupulously accurate and delightfully simple to use – but not generalizable at all; it is only a model of one particular chunk of the UK.

Some social scientists regard the Impostulate as a cop-out – they want to be like the 'hard' sciences – but I think it is how knowledge about complex human systems works. I believe that the model I have presented in this book is pretty accurate, works in a very wide range of situations and is easy to use.

Appendix B: The Big Ideas

These are presented with the year of their Programme's first accession to power (their year of Great Endorsement, where different, is shown in brackets). Those of unfulfilled Aspirant Programmes are in italics.

1905 (1906)
New Liberalism. The poorest people in the UK are trapped in poverty, and only the state can remedy this. We will set up a German-style welfare system to enable them to escape this trap and lead more fulfilling lives. We will pay for it with income and land taxes, not import tariffs, as free trade creates wealth.

1916
The Knock-out Blow. Imperial Germany represents absolute evil, so the War must be fought to the end and won, whatever the price. To do this requires massive state intervention in the economy and ultimate political control of the military.

1918
A Fit Country for Heroes to Live in. Lloyd George's charismatic leadership. Continued Liberal reforms at home, including finally sorting the Irish question. (?)Germany will be punished for the Great War.

1922 (1924)
Tranquillity. Let the nation unite, under Baldwin's gentlemanly, avuncular leadership. Avoiding extremism, we will quietly get on with wealth-creation. Internationally, we will work towards creating a more peaceful world through diplomacy, but there will be as little meddling in foreign affairs as possible.

1940 (1945)

1945 Socialism. The state owns the 'commanding heights of the economy' and provides free education and healthcare. Fair shares for all (hence the need for continued rationing.) The fighting/working man and woman are the new Heroes.

1951 (1955)

Fifties 'One Nation' Conservatism. The Welfare State provides a safety net but no more: people must be free to pursue their own economic success. Old rules: no tinkering with the existing social structure or traditional values (family, patriotism, church etc.)

1964 (1966)

White Heat. Unleashing the power of science and technology, of the potential of planning, of removing the baleful control of the old class system, to create a new Britain, which would not only be more efficient but less stuffy and more open.

1970

Heathism. *(pre-U-turns) Join EC. 'Selsdon' economic freedom.*

1974

The Social Contract. *Unions, CBI and government to co-run Britain. Prices and Incomes policy.*

1979 (1983)

Thatcherism. Take on the unions. No more Keynesian tinkering with levels of demand in the economy: 'supply-side' economics will help businesses thrive and create employment. Promote enterprise, free markets, low tax, small state – at home and abroad (especially in Eastern Europe).

1997

New Labour. An inclusive community where individuals are free to live as they choose. Women's and minority rights asserted. 'Third Way' economy: increased expenditure on public goods to be provided by a mixture of state and private capital.

2010

The Big Society *Decentralize power to responsible citizens – nudge them if they need directing. Socially liberal. The debt must be paid off. Austerity, continued cuts in government spending, is the only way to do that.*

2016 (2019)

Populist 'Brexit' Nationalism. Hard Brexit – as great a distance between ourselves and the European Union as possible. Culture Wars: take political and social power from liberal, metropolitan elites. Johnson's charismatic leadership. (For one wing) Levelling up. (For the other wing) A low-tax, low-regulation, small as possible 'Singapore-on-Thames' state.

?2024

The 21ˢᵗ Century New Deal. We will put our brightest and best minds to work on finding creative and co-operative solutions to our problems. An enabling state will play a key part, creating public goods such as education, mental/physical health and a fair society, and protecting common goods – especially the survival of the planet.

Appendix C: Glossary

<u>Action Group</u>. A small, self-defined group that meets to drive a Political Programme from being a purely intellectual entity to actually having political power. Compare with 'Crucible Group'.

<u>Action Plan.</u> A list of Core Policies, prioritized in order of urgency.

<u>Archetype.</u> A model voter – and potential activist – courted by a Programme.

<u>Ashes (Time of)</u>. The period after a political party has had its latest Programme obliterated. See 'Waterloo'.

<u>Aspirant Political Programme.</u> An Original set of Models, Values, Stories and Core Policies, constellated around a clear, simple Big Idea, that seeks to be Politically Successful.

<u>Big Battle</u>. A struggle with a major interest group whose power is so entrenched that it can only be taken on during a Programme's Pomp.

<u>Big Idea.</u> The essence of a Programme's vision and intention. It can be summed up in a simple sentence, word or phrase, though expanding that to a few sentences can be helpful. This expanded version is like the 'elevator pitch' of a business.

<u>Big Split</u>. A fundamental and irreconcilable disagreement between two sections of a political party, resulting in publicly warring factions.

<u>Big Win</u>. The successful rollout of a Core Policy. It can sometimes also be a highly successful piece of Normal Politics.

<u>Body-blow</u>. An event that seriously and permanently damages the credibility of an administration, kicking away one of its key supports. This can be an event that shows that some element of the Worldview of the Programme is now irrelevant or plain wrong, or it can be a U-turn on a Core Policy.

<u>Broken Programme</u>. One that has suffered a Body-blow.

<u>Canon</u>. A small collection of Sacred Texts.

<u>Carried forward</u> (of a policy). An aspect of one Programme that is also adopted by a subsequent one. Example: the policy of the Welfare State, carried forward from 1945 Socialism to Fifties Conservatism.

<u>Clamping Down</u>. Actions by an undemocratic regime, where it responds to policy failures by violently stifling criticism.

<u>Core Policies</u>. The policies that a Political Programme considers essential. These must be carried out. Major deviations from them (see 'U-turns') are fatal.

<u>Counterblast</u>. A flowering of artistic creativity during a Programme's Pomp, which expresses a radically different Worldview to that of the Programme.

<u>Crowning Glory</u>. A spontaneous national celebration of some kind, which (roughly) coincides with a Programme's Great Endorsement. It is

a (for many people, subconscious) celebration of the Programme's Worldview.

Crucible Group. A small, self-defined group that meets to develop the Models, Values, Stories, Core Policies and Big Idea of a Programme. Compare with 'Action Group'.

Cultural Endorsement. A flowering of artistic creativity around the time of a Programme's Great Endorsement and during its Pomp, which shares and expresses that Programme's Worldview (or much of it).

Cultural Power. The intellectual and emotional resonance of a Programme's Worldview with a large section of the electorate.

Dead Cat Bounce. In financial markets, a short-lived rally in a falling market. I use it as a metaphor for when a broken Programme begins to recover in the polls – because the opposition have yet to come up with a compelling alternative. See 'Drift'.

Dethronement. The moment when a rival Programme gets its First Taste of Power. The dethroned Programme's advocates will be dismissive of this, and will still think they can fight back. Usually, but not always, they are wrong.

Dissolution. The process whereby a once-mighty Political Programme falls apart after its replacement has triumphed in a Great Endorsement.

Drift. A period when one Programme is broken but there is no alternative yet available.

First Big Failure. A major policy error by a Programme, usually late in its Pomp, which begins to erode public confidence in it. "We still like you, but…" Contrast with 'Great Escape' and 'Body-blow'.

First Taste of Power. The moment a Programme becomes responsible (in part, at least) for policy. This can be in coalition, in government but with a tiny majority, or in government with a slightly bigger majority but under a barrage of sustained criticism. The Programme is still 'on approval' from the voters; later it will either be rejected by them or be rewarded with a Great Endorsement.

Foil. The 'number two' to a Leader. Not necessarily with a formal title like Deputy PM, but the person with whom they work in tandem to create and/or deliver the Programme.

Founder. A member of a Programme's Crucible or Action Groups.

Great Endorsement. A Landslide electoral victory. 100 seats or more, ideally. Certainly 60 or more. It is the achievement of this that turns an Aspirant Political Programme into a fully-fledged one.

Great Escape. A major policy error by a Programme early in its Pomp, which the public forgives, because it still believes strongly in the Programme and shares its Worldview (sufficiently, anyway).

Leader. The driving individual force of a Political Programme, who becomes party leader then PM. They may not be in place right at the start of things, but can rise to the surface as the Programme develops.

Limping Along. What a Political Programme does after it has received a Body-blow. See 'Broken Programme'.

Normal Politics. The creation of policies that are not Core, in response to unexpected events after the Programme has achieved power. Unlike Core policies, Normal policies can be reversed, and should be if they aren't working.

Palace Revolution. A change of Political Programme caused by personnel and ideological changes within a ruling party. In democracies, these still need endorsement at the ballot box (during wartime, this endorsement has to wait).

Political Programme. An Original, Timely and Politically Successful set of Models, Values, Stories and Core Policies, constellated around a clear, simple Big Idea.

Politically Successful. A Programme is Politically Successful if it achieves a Landslide victory. See 'Great Endorsement'.

Pomp. The period after a Programme has received a Great Endorsement. During this time, the Programme is 'Teflon-coated', and has the time and space to realize its Action Plan.

Positive Feedback Loop. In systems theory, this is a cycle of interacting self-reinforcing causes, which leads to an effect growing ever more substantial. This cycle just builds and builds, until some external event interrupts the pattern. The term 'positive' is misleading: this is a technical term and carries no moral approbation. The opposite, 'negative feedback', is a cycle where the interacting causes in some way correct one another, leading to stability.

The terms 'virtuous circle' and 'vicious circle' are sometimes used to approve or disapprove of a Positive Feedback Loop's direction of travel – but even here, there are technical overtones: virtuous circles create complex entities; vicious circles smash them apart.

Replacement Leader. A leader who takes over after the fall of a full-on Political Programme Leader. Examples: Arthur Balfour, Neville Chamberlain, Alec Douglas-Home, John Major, Gordon Brown, Rishi Sunak.

Representative Democracy. Our current system, with general elections every five years or so, which return MPs, one for each constituency. Contrasted on one side with ideas like 'direct democracy', which means regular referenda on major issues, and on the other with authoritarianism (rigged elections, autocratic leaders, dissent stifled).

Sacred Text. A text that has had an essential formative influence on a Programme.

Significant Influence. The moment when the Leader of an Aspirant Political Programme achieves a position of influence, usually as Leader of the Opposition.

Slogan. An eye-catching way of drawing attention to what is special about a Programme. (By contrast, the Big Idea is what actually is special.)

Slow Strangler. A problem that comes up again and again (and again and again), but which a Programme is helpless to solve because of its ideological blinkers.

Stories. The two types of narrative at the heart of a Political Programme. Those of the First type, Slaying the Dragon, are about how negative, damaging things will be swept away. The Second type tell how a Bright Future will be built once this has happened.

Triumphalism. An unnecessary, hubristic 'rubbing the old enemy's face in it' at the start of a Programme's Pomp.

U-turn. The abandonment or reversal of a Core Policy.

Villain. In a Programme's First Stories, the malign force, or an individual or organization serving it, from which the country has to be freed.

Waterloo. The moment when a Programme knows it is truly defeated.

Worldview. A Programme's (or a voter's) Models, Values and Stories.

Zeitgeist. A deep swell of public perception of, and opinion on, major political, moral and cultural issues. Various people have been credited with the invention of the term, all around the late 18th and early 19th centuries.

Appendix D: UK General Election Results, 1906 - 2019

Year	Winner	Leader	Maj	
1906	Liberals	Henry Campbell-Bannerman	129	Great Endorsement of New Liberalism
1910	(Liberals)	HH Asquith	-	Minority government
1910	(Liberals)	HH Asquith	-	Minority government
1918	Coalition	David Lloyd George	283	Great Endorsement of 2nd LG administration
1922	Cons	Andrew Bonar Law	74	First Taste of Power for Tranquillity
1923	(Lab)	Ramsay Macdonald	-	Minority gov't. Aspirant PP fails to take off
1924	Cons	Stanley Baldwin	210	Great Endorsement for Tranquillity
1929	(Lab)	Ramsay Macdonald	-	Minority gov't. Second attempt by Aspirant PP, also fails
1931	National	Ramsay Macdonald	492	Huge underlying Cons majority makes this a continuation of the Tranquillity Programme
1935	National	Stanley Baldwin	242	As above
1945	Lab	Clement Attlee	146	Great Endorsement of 1945 Socialism
1950	Lab	Clement Attlee	5	
1951	Cons	Winston Churchill	17	First Taste of Power for Fifties Conservatism
1955	Cons	Anthony Eden	60	Great Endorsement of Fifties Conservatism

1959	Cons	Harold Macmillan	100	
1964	Lab	Harold Wilson	4	First Taste of Power for White Heat
1966	Lab	Harold Wilson	98	Great Endorsement for White Heat
1970	Cons	Ted Heath	30	Dethronement of White Heat
1974	(Lab)	Harold Wilson	-	Minority government
1974	Lab	Harold Wilson	3	First Taste of Power for Aspirant Social Contract
1979	Cons	Margaret Thatcher	43	First Taste of Power for Thatcherism
1983	Cons	Margaret Thatcher	144	Great Endorsement of Thatcherism
1987	Cons	Margaret Thatcher	102	
1992	Cons	John Major	21	
1997	Lab	Tony Blair	179	Great Endorsement of New Labour
2001	Lab	Tony Blair	167	
2005	Lab	Tony Blair	66	
2010	Coalition	David Cameron	78	… but no overall majority for any party (Cons 307, Lab 258, LD 57, Rest 28)
2015	Cons	David Cameron	12	
2017	(Cons)	Theresa May	-	Minority government
2019	Cons	Boris Johnson	80	Great Endorsement of Populist 'Brexit' Nat'ism

Appendix E
The Body-blows

At the opposite end of the story from the victories above, here is a list of Body-blows received by the various Programmes described in this book. Most of them fall into the first category, which is…

Ones from which Programmes Never Recovered.

New Liberalism
WW1 not 'over by Christmas', but instead quickly became a horrendous, static war of attrition.

Lloyd George 2 – a Fit Country for Heroes
Geddes Axe.

Tranquillity
Hitler's annexation of the whole of Czechoslovakia, March 1939.

Fifties Conservatism
Profumo Affair, 1962/3.

White Heat
Devaluation of the pound, 1967

Heathism
1974 miners' strike.

The Social Contract
Winter of Discontent, 1978/9.

Thatcherism
Black Wednesday, 1992.

New Labour
2007/8 Financial Crisis.

The Coalition (Lib Dems)
Tripling of Tuition Fees, 2010.

Populist Brexit Nationalism
Truss/Kwarteng fiasco, 2022.

Programmes that, instead of Receiving a Fatal Body-blow, were Destroyed by other Forces

Salisbury/Balfour Programme of 1895 (Big Split over free trade vs. tariffs)

1945 Socialism (Slowly Strangled by rationing, with Big Split at the end).

The Coalition (Conservatives) (Slowly Strangled by austerity)

Programmes that Simply Ended, Job Done

Lloyd George 1 – 'The Knock-out Blow'

Appendix F
The Eras: A Playlist

The spirits of eras are sometimes hard to put into words. Here's a playlist of music that might do the job better.

New Liberalism: Igor Stravinsky, *The Firebird*
I could have chosen something more obviously Edwardian, but the New Liberals liked high culture, and were keen that as many people as possible could rise to its level. This beautiful modernist piece delighted London concertgoers in 1912.

Lloyd George 1: *It's a Long Way to Tipperary*
Lloyd George would no doubt have preferred something more warlike. But the men actually marching off to do the fighting thought more of home than glory.

Lloyd George 2: The Original Dixieland Jazz Band, *Tiger Rag*
The restless, uprooted energy of the immediate post-war era.

Tranquillity: Ralph Vaughan Williams, *The Lark Ascending*
The Programme sought calmness. 'Baldwinism set to music.'

1945 Socialism: Vera Lynn, *We'll meet again*
All pulling together to ensure victory for the new People's Britain.

Fifties 'One Nation' Conservatism: Doris Day, *Que Sera, Sera*; Melodi Light Orchestra *Puffin' Billy*
Keep it light and cheerful after the horrors of war.

'White Heat' Modernization: The Beatles, *A Hard Day's Night*
'Hey, Mister, can we have our ball back?'

The Seventies: Yes, playing as intro to their set, *Finale* from *The Firebird*
As well as entertaining fans, the band's guitarist Steve Howe wanted to introduce them to beautiful classics. This aesthetic ambitiousness speaks of the culture of the early part of this unusual decade. Modern populists, no doubt, would not wish to be lectured by this expert.

Thatcherism: *Rio*, by Duran Duran
Young men on the make and proud of it.

New Labour: Paul Oakenfold, Live at Glastonbury, 2000
Music for a new era, from a place where that era would be celebrated.

Populist 'Brexit' Nationalism: Vera Lynn, duet with Katharine Jenkins, *We'll Meet Again*
Nostalgia was a key part of the Programme's strong emotional appeal to its supporters.

Finally, I can't resist a theme tune for the entire process. *O Fortuna*, from Carl Orff's *Carmina Burana.* Political Programmes rise; Political Programmes fall…

I started compiling this as an amusement, but found doing so oddly thought-provoking and resonant, so include it here. If you have a different set of pieces, do please email me with your list (chris@chriswest.info).

221

Principal References

<u>Electoral Majorities.</u> Sources differ on precise figures. Some calculations include the Speaker; others don't. Independent candidates muddy the waters, too. I have used the figures that I have seen most often cited. The most-debatable figure is that for Lloyd George's Coalition in 1918: my source here is the invaluable *British Electoral Facts, 1832 – 2012*.

<u>Poll data.</u> I use Dr Mark Pack's brilliant *PollBase* (www.markpack.org.)

<u>Specific points</u>
Exhaustive lists of references for every asserted fact, however widely known, seem wasteful. We have trees to preserve! Below, I cite some sources of quotes/facts that are obscure or could be questioned/seen as controversial, or works that readers might want to follow up.

P1. *Blue Ocean Strategy* by W Chan Kim and Renée Mauborgne (Harvard Business Review Press)

p3. *How Brands Become Icons* by Douglas B Holt (Harvard Business Review Press), page 45

p10. Enoch Powell quote. Question in parliament to PM, 6 Nov 1972

p16. Lakatos' piece is in *Criticism and the Growth of Knowledge* (Cambridge University Press)

p27. An interesting book on the genesis of new ideas is *Where Good Ideas Come From*, by Steven Johnson (Riverhead Books)

p27. Katherine Philips on diversity:
https://greatergood.berkeley.edu/article/item/how_diversity_makes_us_smarter

p29. See *Crossing the Chasm*, by Geoffrey Moore (Capstone).

P32. Piece on 'Zeitgeist Leadership' in *Harvard Business Review*, October 2005

p46. 'More a whimper than a bang'. Heppell, T and Theakston, K, (eds.) How Labour Governments Fall: From Ramsay Macdonald to Gordon Brown (Palgrave Macmillan). Available online at https://eprints.whiterose.ac.uk/85710/2/

p66. Quote on the Rite of Spring. 'Primitive Sounds' by Rachel Howerton, *Journal of Musicological Research*, Volume 38, 2019

p75. Loss of popularity of *Belgium put the Kybosh*... See Martin Pegler, *Soldiers' Songs and Slang of the Great War* (Osprey Books)

p98. 'Attlee louder and clearer than Churchill'. See John Bew, *Citizen Clem* (Riverrun), page 222

p109. Macmillan quote from Alistair Horne, *Macmillan* (Macmillan)

p111. 'Colour bar' at Euston: http://news.bbc.co.uk/onthisday/hi/dates/stories/july/15/newsid_3043000/3043439.stm

p111. No Boccaccio in Swindon! https://www.swindonadvertiser.co.uk/news/13720727.rewind-bid-to-ban-filthy-book-in-swindon/

p134. Plenty of people have made the punk/entrepreneur link. E.g. https://the8percent.com/the-punk-rock-guide-to-entrepreneurship/

p134. Jack Jones and Gallup Poll. Lots of references. For example... https://www.theguardian.com/global/2009/apr/22/union-leader-jack-jones-dies

p137. CO2 emissions in UK (and other countries) over time:

https://www.macrotrends.net/countries/GBR/united-kingdom/carbon-co2-emissions

p149. Tory 'sleaze' in 1990s: https://www.independent.co.uk/life-style/sleaze-the-list-1592762.html

p157. '2 million lifted out of poverty' from Matt Beech and Simon Lee (eds), *Ten Years of New Labour* (AIAA)

P160. There are plenty of references to the 'productivity slump' post-2008. *The challenge of unlocking the UK's low productivity* from the FT, by Delphine Strauss, 8 Oct 2021, has some good graphs. See also *Stagnation Nation*, published by The Resolution Foundation

p160. Gordon Brown to Gillian Duffy:
https://www.theguardian.com/politics/2010/apr/28/gordon-brown-gillian-duffy-transcript

p177. Johnson, COBRA and handshakes: *British Medical Journal*: https://www.bmj.com/content/bmj/376/bmj.o273.full.pdf

p178. Brexit losing business:
https://www.cer.eu/insights/cost-brexit-june-2022

p179. Johnson and deceitfulness:
https://www.nytimes.com/2022/07/08/world/europe/boris-johnson-lies-britain-parliament.html and sources quoted in that piece.

p181. Recent (December 2022) polls on Brexit:
https://whatukthinks.org/eu/questions/in-highsight-do-you-think-britain-was-right-or-wrong-to-vote-to-leave-the-eu/

https://www2.politicalbetting.com/index.php/archives/2022/12/10/views-of-brexit-the-age-and-gender-splits/

p183. Kier Starmer, speech at *New Statesman* 'Politics Live' event, 28 June 2022.

p183. For an analysis of the Red Wall, see Sebastian Payne's *Broken Heartlands* (Macmillan)

p184. An analysis of the effectiveness of government outsourcing is the September 2019 report by the Institute of Government. https://www.instituteforgovernment.org.uk/sites/default/files/publications/government-outsourcing-reform-WEB_0.pdf

P185. The work of the Stockholm Resilience Centre is described in *Breaking Boundaries, The Science of Our Planet* (DK)

p201. The topic of algorithms and bubbles was dealt with in Stuart Russell's fascinating 2021 Reith Lectures. www.bbc.co.uk

p221. Steve Howe's desire to 'educate' fans: https://www.yesworld.com/yesshows-the-opening-music/firebird-suite-excerpt-finale/

Acknowledgements

I hope you have enjoyed this book and found it stimulating. Any comments or thoughts would be hugely appreciated. My email is chris@chriswest.info.

Books are always team efforts. Special thanks to…

Graham Michelli, who suggested the concept of the Big Idea as the key to serious electoral victory.

Gervas Huxley at Bristol University, who went through an earlier draft with great thoroughness and expertise. We've also had loads of phone conversations, which have been invaluable.

David Willetts, who made some hugely helpful comments on an earlier draft (and provided a positive quote).

Dr Mark Pack's *Pollbase* has been a great resource, provided free.

Justin Mendez, Sheena Siega-Alinson and the team at 100covers.com, who have been very patient with my repeated requests for 'tweaks' to the book cover. Customer service as it should be!

My wife, Rayna, and my daughter, Imogen, for long conversations on various topics in this book over the dinner table or on car journeys.

Printed in Great Britain
by Amazon

18365523R00139